PICKLEBALL FOR BEGINNERS

LEARN HOW TO PLAY PICKLEBALL WITH PICKLEBALL BASICS, RULES, TECHNIQUES, AND STRATEGIES TO MASTER THE GAME

TYSON JOHNS

PUBLISHING FORTE

INTRODUCTION

Pickleball is a fantastic combination of exercise, social connection, and fun. It's simple to see why pickleball is the fastest emerging sport in the United States after you try it.

Pickleball was founded in 1965 by Joel Pritchard, Bill Bell, and Barney McCallum. The inventors aimed to prevent the largest or quickest players from dominating the game. It was also designed to be a communal game for amusement and family enjoyment. There are currently over 2.5 million players in the United States.

This book is intended to assist new players in becoming acquainted with the game. Experience is a terrific instructor, but having a working grasp of the rules, fundamental techniques, and frequent mistakes made by novice players is also beneficial. This book is also meant to assist experienced players in advancing their game by remaining anchored in the fundamentals.

The first chapter covers everything about Pickleball, including the game's history and how it came to be played. The second chapter covers the basics, such as the necessary equipment and court dimensions.

The third chapter covers getting started, including how to hold the paddle and hit the ball. The fourth chapter covers techniques, such as how to serve and return the ball. The fifth chapter covers strategies, such as where to place your shots and how to set up a point. The sixth chapter covers mistakes to avoid, such as not keeping your eye on the ball or not following through with your swing.

The seventh chapter covers the World Pickleball Games, which is the sport's premier event. These games are held every year in different locations around the world. The eighth chapter covers how to practice by yourself or with a partner. And finally, the ninth chapter covers health and safety, such as how to stay hydrated and avoid injuries.

1
ALL ABOUT PICKLEBALL

Pickleball is an excellent paddle sport that can be played indoors and outdoors by all ages. The game is played with a paddle-like tennis table and a plastic ball.

IN THIS CHAPTER, we will discuss the history of the sport, the benefits of playing it, and why it's so popular.

What is Pickleball?

Did you know that pickleball is one of the fastest-growing sports in the United States? This paddle sport is a fun, competitive, and social game for all ages and is a mix of tennis, badminton, and table tennis. pickleball is played on courts 20 feet wide by 44 feet long, with a net 36 inches high at the center.

. . .

UNLIKE TENNIS or other net games, service in pickleball is underhand, and you aim to alternate between service boxes. Volleys are allowed, but players cannot touch the ball twice in succession.

The History of Pickleball

History of the year 1965

Joel Pritchard, a congressman from state of Washington, and Bill Bell, a prosperous businessman, drove to Pritchard's house on Bain-bridge-Island (close to Seattle) after a Saturday of golf, to see their households lounging about with nothing else to do. Bell and Pritchard searched the property for some badminton stuff to use the ancient badminton court, but they could not locate a complete set of those rackets. They adjusted and began playing using ping pong-paddles and a plastic ball that had holes punched into it. In the beginning, they kicked the ball above the net at the standard height of sixty inches.

AS THE WEEKEND WENT ON, the ball bounced nicely on the surface of the asphalt, and the net line was soon reduced to thirty-six inches. At Pritchard's house the next weekend evening, Barney Mc-Callum was given his first taste of the game. Soon, all these three guys established rules that extensively included badminton. They stayed true to the original intent, which was to offer a sport the entire household could enjoy together.

HISTORY of the year 1967

In the garden of Bob O'Brian, a neighbor and friend of

Joel Pritchard, the very 1st permanent pickleball court was built.

History *of the year 1972*

A corporation was established to safeguard the development of this newly established game or sport.

History *of the year 1975*

The pickleball article that appeared in the National-Observer was followed by one on 'America's very newest sport of racquet' in Tennis sports magazine in 1976.

History *of the year 1976*

The first pickleball battle ever recorded occurred at the South-Center-Athletic-Club in Tukwila, Dc, in the springtime of 1976. Men's Singles champion David Lester has won and Steve-Paranto in second. College tennis players who understood very little about pickleball made up a large portion of participants. They practiced with a plastic ball that was the size of a softball and big wooden paddles.

History *of the year 1978*

Pickleball information was provided in the book named The Other-Racquet-Sports.

History *of the year 1982*

Sid Williams was a pickleball founder who started playing & running competitions in DC Washington State.

. . .

HISTORY *of the year 1984*

To maintain the expansion and improvement of pickleball gameplay on a national scale, the (U.S.A.P.A.) United-States-Amateur-Pickleball-Association was established. In March of 1984, the 1st rulebook was printed.

SID WILLIAMS SERVED as the organization's first president and executive director from 1984 until 1998. Frank-Candelario took up as his successor and continued activities until 2004.

BOEING-INDUSTRIAL-ENGINEER ARLEN PARANTO created the 1st ever composite paddle. He used the Nomex or fiberglass honeycomb panels that airline companies employ for their aircraft's structural system and flooring. Until Arlen sold the business to Frank-Candelario, he produced roughly 1,000 paddles out of materials, including honeycomb or a fiberglass core and honeycomb or a graphite core.

HISTORY *of the year 1990*

Pickleball games were going on in all of the 50 states.

HISTORY *of the year 1992*

Using a special drilling machine, Pickle-Ball-Inc. produced pickleball within the house.

HISTORY *of the year 1997*

At the age of 72, Joel Pritchard died away. Even though he served as the lieutenant governor of Washington State from

1988 until 1996, he is likely most recognized for his involvement in the invention of pickleball.

HISTORY *of the year 1999*
Pickleball Stuff, the very first pickleball website ever founded, offered players information, products and equipment.

HISTORY *of the year 2001*
Earl Hill worked hard to include pickleball in the Arizona-Senior Olympics for the first time. There were 100 participants in the competition, which was held in RV Happy Trails Resort in Surprise, Arizona. The size of the event was unmatched at the time. About 300 players participated in the tournament over the next several years.

HISTORY *of the year 2003*
The Pickleball-Stuff website lists 39 well-known locations to play the game in North of America. This includes around 150 different courts as well as 10 States and 3 provinces of Canada.

THE HUNTSMAN-WORLD-SENIOR-GAMES, held annually in the St. George, Ut., in the month of October, featured pickleball for the very first time.

HISTORY *of the year 2005*

The (USAPA) USA Association of Pickleball is a brand-new organization devoted to the sport. The first president was Mark Friedenberg, and the inaugural Board-of-Directors for the newly formed USAPA contained the following individuals:

- Fran Myer was the secretary
- Steve Wong was the vice president
- Lela Reed was the treasurer
- Phil Mortenson was the grievance
- Phil Mortenson was the general counsel
- Marketing - Pat Carroll in March 2006, then Erne Perry
- Earl Hill was the Ambassador Program and International or National Relations
- Carole Myers was the membership
- Jettye Lanius was the newsletter
- Dennis Duey was the rules teller
- Mark Friedenberg was the rankings & rating teller
- Barney Myer was the tournaments teller
- Steve Wong was the webmaster
- Norm Davis was the trainer

The initial USAPA website was developed by former Webmaster of USAPA, Steve Wong and launched in March. The growth of the pickleball gameplay and the expansion of the website's functions both contributed to a rise in the website's activity. On the 1st of July, USAPA had become Non-profitable-corporation.

To provide a single trustworthy resource for gamers to locate gaming sites, USAPA worked with several sites to just have them stop offering Sites to Play their links and combine all of the information into USAPA's database. Its current link is places2play.org.

History of the year 2006
Bill Bell, one of the sport's original pioneers, died at the age of 83.

History of the year 2008
The Association of Pickleball Official-Tournament-Rulebook USA- Revision: on May 1st, 2008, was authorized by the Rules Committee of USAPA, which was led by a person named Dennis Duey.

For the very first time, pickleball was offered at the (NSGA) National Senior Association of Games.

The website of USAPA now lists 420 venues for play in the North America. This covers around 1500 separate courts and 4 provinces of Canada & 43 states. The addition of courts inside private residences is not taken into account by this.

. . .

PICKLEBALL WAS the subject of a live, within-studio program on the channel Good-Morning-ABC's-America that also included a quick demo. This was actually the sport's very first major media presentation.

History of the year 2009

In Buckeye, located in Arizona, from November 2 to 8, 2009, the inaugural National Tournament of USAPA for all ages of players was conducted. Nearly 400 athletes from twenty-six states & numerous provinces of Canada participated in the competition.

TO HELP players build new sites for further new players, USAPA develops the program of Grant. More than 1,400 additional sites were accounted for by the program at the closing of 2013.

History of the year 2010

USAPA founded the (IFP) International Pickleball Federation organization and associated website to aid in the development of the game on a global scale.

History of the year 2013

Justin Maloof started working with USAPA as the organization's 1st full-time Director of Executives in January. The USAPA had 4,071 members to begin the year, which is a record.

. . .

A VERY NEW logo and blue, white, & red color scheme, which is more in line with some other US local sports regulatory organizations, are used by USAPA in its rebranding.

History *of the year 2014*

USAPA established a brand-new, user-friendly internet site.

PICKLEBALL CHANNEL WAS the first dedicated sports media network when it initially emerged.

History *of the year 2015*

USAPA has more than 10,000 of members for a very first time. In the city of Tahoe located in California, the inaugural ambassador retreat of USAPA took place.

THERE ARE CURRENTLY SLIGHTLY over two million pickleball players, in accordance with the (SFIA) Fitness & Sports Industry Association.

MASTER YOUR BASICS, Compete with the Confidence and Pickleball Fundamentals is the modern pickleball handbook for the beginners produced by the author named Mary Littlewood, publisher named Human Kinetics & USAPA.

THE NATIONAL CHAMPIONSHIPS of USAPA are moved to the Casa Grande in Arizona by USAPA after six years in Arizona, Buckeye. Places2Play's total no of courts is increasing, surpassing 10,000 of courts and ending the year with 12,800 for outdoor as well as indoor courts.

HISTORY *of the year 2016*
   According to USAPA, it presently has over 17,000 participants. USAPA develops a program of nationwide qualified referee certification.

PICKLEBALL MAGAZINE PREMIERED as the very first expert print, full color and web magazine for the sport. Members of USAPA are entitled to a discounted subscription fee as well as a free web copy.

IN NAPLES, Florida, during the inaugural Open US Pickleball Championships, pickleball was broadcasted for the very first time on CBS-Sports Channel. The number of sites on Places2Play has increased to around 4,600.

USAPA CHOOSES Jude St. Children's Hospital for Research as the official national charity partner.

THE USAPA JOINS with the Senior Super International Association of Pickleball (SSIPA), which was founded, to regulate all of its competitions.

HISTORY *of the year 2017*
   Over 1,500 volunteers make up the USAPA Ambassador

organization. On Places2Play, there are around 5,900 sites. The number of regionals of USAPA rises from 8 to 11.

THE ASSOCIATION OF AMERICAN BUILDERS SPORTS (ASBA) and USAPA collaborated to write the first book on pickleball court building that is authorized by the sports sector. The construction and maintenance of pickleball courts are covered in depth in the manual Pickleball Courts, which is actually a maintenance and construction manual.

A HALL OF FAME FOR PICKLEBALL was established by the USAPA & also the International Association of Teaching Professional Pickleball (IPTPA). Barney McCallum, Joel Pritchard, Sid Williams, Mark Friedenberg, Billy Jacobsen and Arlen Paranto were the first inductees. The National Championships of USAPA broke participation records with over of 1,300 athletes, & for the very first time, a two-hour portion of the competition was set to air to a statewide audience on the channel CBS Network of Sports. In 2 years, membership of USAPA doubled, reaching 22,000 until December.

HISTORY *of the year 2018*
Over 30,000 people are members of USAPA. There are around 7,000 total courts at Places2Play sites, while there are approximately 21,000 courts in total in the United States.

THE 1ST (UTPRs) tournament results-based player ratings in the sport are produced and launched by USAPA in collaboration with Pickleballtournaments.com.

. . .

THE NEWLY ESTABLISHED PPR Pickleball Professional Registry, a PTR Tennis Professional Registry division, and USAPA are partners. PPR certifies more than 1,000 pickleball teachers in the very first six months.

THE FIRST HISTORY of the game was co-written and published by USAPA members Beverly Youngren and Jennifer Lucore under the title "History of Pickleball-And Over 50 Years of Fun".

THE WORLD NATIONAL Championships are currently held in the legendary Tennis Garden located in the Indian Wells, California, thanks to a multi-year partnership between the Pickleball USA Association & LLC. Desert Champions. Over 2,200 people have registered for the newly renamed USA Pickleball Margaritaville National Championships. A 60-minute clip from the event was broadcast nationally on the channel ESP-NEWS; more than 17 hrs. of live footage were streamed to an audience across the country on the channel ESPN3. The competition offers the greatest cash prize in sport's history of $75,000 as well.

THE TEAM of USAPA Facebook broadcasts multiple National Championships live matches on Facebook, reaching approximately more than 1.5 million audiences in total. Earl Hill, Robert Lanius & Fran Myer were all inducted into the hall-of-fame for pickleball.

History of the year 2019

As a part of its expansion strategy, the Pickleball Association of USA hired several new employees, including Karen Parrish, the chief of officiating and competition. George Bauernfeind, the 1st Marketing Chief Officer, and Hope Tolley, the managing director of recreation programs. Pickleball continues to be one of the sports with the highest growth in the United States, according to the report of 2019's Fitness Sports Industry Association, which includes 3.3 million players.

BARNEY MCCALLUM, the third and last original pioneer of this sport, died at the age of 93. The USA Pickleball Margaritaville National Championships give spectators, as well as the experience of spectators, more of a priority. Beyond the stadium court, live TV screens and a VIP lounge were set up so spectators could watch the proceedings from the beverage and food sections. Nearly 28,000 individuals attended the event.

STEVE PARANTO, Dan Gabanek, Enrique Ruiz, and Jennifer Lucore were all inducted into the hall of fame for pickleball. By year's end, USAPA had about 40,000 members, an increase of 1,000% from the start of 2013.

History of the year 2020

To better correspond with other sports of US regulatory bodies, including the Pickleball USA National Championships, USAPA changed its name to USA Pickleball. A fresh website and a new, contemporary logo are also part of the brand's relaunch. The updated name, website, and logo are intended to enhance USA Pickleball's reputation as the national pickleball association of the United States. In

December, Stu Upson was hired as the organization's very 1st CEO of full-time.

History *of the year 2021*

With just more than 53,000 members at the conclusion of the year, a 43 percent gain from the prior year and the organization's highest single expansion year to the date, Pickleball USA Membership surpassed the 50,000 mark. The 2021 USA Pickleball Margaritaville National Championships hosted by Central Pickleball was the biggest event to date, with more than 2,300 participants enrolled.

USAPA KEPT up its investment in personnel infrastructure and had approximately 20 employees by year's end. Numerous national segments on CNBC, NBC's The Show of Today, BBC News & Live with Ryan n Kelly, as well as articles published in prestigious magazines like Vanity Fair, The Times of New York, Forbes, The Globe Boston, Allure, The Economist, Sports Illustrated, USA Today, Parade, as well as Axios, all helped to raise awareness.

The Benefits of Playing Pickleball

In addition to being a fun and social game, pickleball also offers several health benefits. A good workout is one of the main reasons why people play pickleball. The sport gives you a great cardio workout and can also help to improve balance and coordination.

Here are some other benefits of playing pickleball:

1. Boosts Cardiovascular Health

A recent study by the University of Arizona found that pickleball can help to improve cardiovascular health. The study found that pickleball players had lower heart rates and blood pressure levels than those who didn't play the game. this is likely because pickleball is a high-energy, low-impact sport.

In addition, the pickleball players also had better arterial stiffness and left ventricular function. These findings suggest that playing pickleball can help to reduce the risk of cardiovascular disease.

2. Lowers Risk of Diabetes

Pickleball is a great workout because it increases your heart rate and makes you move your whole body. A study in the Journal of Diabetes Research found that pickleball can lower your risk of type 2 diabetes. The study looked at more than 700 adults aged 50 and over. The participants were divided into two groups: those who played pickleball regularly and those who didn't play any sports. The study found that the pickleball players had a lower risk of type 2 diabetes than the non-athletes.

IN ADDITION to boosting cardiovascular health, pickleball can also help to lower the risk of type 2 diabetes. Pickleball can help to improve insulin sensitivity and blood sugar levels. This is likely because playing Pickleball increases muscle mass and reduces body fat. Combining these factors can help improve insulin sensitivity and lower the risk of type 2 diabetes.

3. Improves Balance and Coordination

PICKLEBALL IS a great way to improve balance and coordination. The game requires quick movements and sudden changes in direction. This helps to improve proprioception, which is the ability to sense the position of your body in space. Proprioception is critical for balance. In addition, Pickleball also helps to improve hand-eye coordination and fine motor skills.

THE GAME REQUIRES players to hit a small ball with a paddle. You have to move quickly and accurately to hit the ball. Pickleball also requires players to use fine motor skills to control the paddle. These skills can transfer to other activities, such as driving a car or using a computer. The improved hand-eye coordination and fine motor skills can also help to reduce the risk of falls.

4. Reduces Stress Levels

FOR MANY PICKLEBALL PLAYERS, reduced stress levels are one of the primary benefits of playing pickleball. The game is relatively low intensity, and it's easy to stay in control of the ball and your movements. As a result, Pickleball can be a great way to unwind after a long day or week. It's also an excellent way to boost your spirits.

IN ADDITION, the social interaction that comes with playing pickleball can help reduce stress levels by providing a sense of connection and community. And finally, the simple act of being outdoors and moving your body can also help lower stress hormone levels.

5. Improves Bone Density

PLAYING pickleball can also help to improve bone density. This is especially beneficial for older adults at a higher risk for osteoporosis. Studies have shown that pickleball can help increase bone density in men and women of all ages.

MUSCLE MASS ALSO IMPROVES, which has the spinoff of helping support and protect bones. Combining these two factors can help reduce the risk of osteoporosis and improve bone density. As a result, pickleball is an ideal way to stay active and improve your bone health.

6. Boosts Brain Health

PLAYING pickleball helps to boost brain health. The game requires quick thinking and strategic planning, and studies have shown that this can help to improve cognitive function. Pickleball also helps improve coordination and balance, both of which are important for brain health.

AS PEOPLE AGE, they often experience a decline in cognitive function and balance. Pickleball can help to delay or prevent this decline, making it an excellent way to stay mentally sharp as you age. Not only can it help to improve cognitive function, but it can also help to reduce the risk of falls and improve brain health.

7. Improves Sleep Quality

MOST PEOPLE KNOW that exercise is important for maintaining good health, but many don't realize that exercising can have different effects on the body. Pickleball seems to be especially effective at improving deep sleep, which is the type of sleep that is most restorative.

DURING DEEP SLEEP, the body repairs tissues to support brain function and boosts immunity. In addition, deep sleep is critical for reducing stress levels. People who get enough deep sleep are also less likely to suffer from anxiety and depression.

8. Reduces Joint Pain

BEING A LOW-IMPACT SPORT, it puts less stress on your joints than other activities like running or basketball. As a result, Pickleball is an excellent way to stay active if you have joint pain or other joint-related problems.

PLAYING the game can be an especially good way for older adults to stay active and reduce joint pain. And for people with conditions like arthritis, it can provide much-needed relief from pain and stiffness. The low-impact nature of the sport makes it an ideal way to stay active without aggravating joint pain.

9. Increases Muscle Strength

PLAYING REGULARLY, you'll notice your muscle strength increasing significantly, which is so important in supporting and protecting joints. Pickleball can help to improve upper body strength, lower body strength, and grip strength. And because pickleball is a weight-bearing exercise, it can also help prevent bone loss.

. . .

During Pickleball, players use a variety of strokes to hit the ball. These strokes help to focus on different muscle groups, and as a result, Pickleball also helps in ton and strengthen muscles all over the body. Whether you're looking to improve your fitness or just want to have some fun, pickleball is a great option.

10. Increases Flexibility

Most people know that playing sports is good for their health, but did you know that pickleball can help to improve your flexibility? That's right - this relatively new sport is perfect for those looking to increase their range of motion. Pickleball is easy on the joints, meaning that players can stay active without putting too much strain on their bodies.

This makes it an excellent activity for seniors or those with joint problems. In addition, the back-and-forth motion of pickleball helps to loosen up tight muscles, making it an excellent way to improve flexibility.

The Popularity of Pickleball

In the United States, the popularity of pickleball has grown exponentially in recent years. According to the Sports & Fitness Industry Association, the number of pickleball players in the US rose from 2.8 million in 2013 to 3.5 million in 2020. And this trend shows no signs of slowing down. In 2023, the number of pickleball players in the US is expected to reach 4.8 million.

. . .

Many experts believe that pickleball will continue to grow in popularity due to its low barriers to entry. pickleball is a relatively inexpensive sport to get into, and it can be played on a variety of surfaces, including tennis courts, badminton courts, and even in your backyard. The equipment used in pickleball is also relatively simple and can be easily transported to different locations.

While the sport is growing in popularity, it's still relatively unknown. This means that there are plenty of opportunities for people to get involved in pickleball. So, if you're looking for a new and exciting way to stay active, pickleball may be just what you're looking for.

Why You Should Start Playing

This chapter discussed some of the many reasons you should start playing pickleball, including the fact that it is a low-impact sport that is easy on the joints and can help improve muscle mass and bone density. When it comes to health benefits, pickleball has a lot to offer. It is an excellent way to increase flexibility.

Pickleball is an excellent way to reduce joint pain, improve muscle strength, and increase flexibility. The game is also easy to learn and can be played by people of all ages and skill levels. Pickleball is also growing in popularity, making it a great way to meet new people and make new friends. So pickleball is worth checking out if you're looking for a fun and challenging way to improve your health.

2
BASICS AND FUNDAMENTALS OF PICKLEBALL GAME

This chapter will teach you the basics of the game, from the court layout to the scoring system. By the end of this chapter, you'll be ready to hit the courts and start playing! While pickleball may seem confusing at first, with a little practice, you'll be playing like a pro in no time.

Pickleball Equipment and Court Layout

Pickleball is a fun and easy sport to get into, and it can be played with just a few simple pieces of equipment.

1. Paddle

PICKLEBALL PADDLES COME in various sizes and shapes, but they all have one common goal: to help you play your best game of pickleball. You should keep a few things in mind when choosing a paddle, such as the weight, grip, and material. The paddle's weight will affect your arm's fatigue, so choosing one that feels comfortable is crucial. The grip is also important - you want one that will provide a good grip without being too slippery.

Choosing a Pickleball Paddle

Paddles in general

IF YOU ARE brand new to pickleball, or considering buying your first paddle, there are many things that you should consider when selecting the right paddle for you. With the explosive growth of pickleball, the technology, brands, and styles of paddles are rapidly changing and are cropping up more and more in sporting goods and large box retailers around the world.

THE FIRST PICKLEBALL paddles were made from a single piece of wood, which now seems like ancient technology as paddles nowadays are made of more sophisticated materials such as polymer honeycomb cores and graphite carbon fiber composites. In reality, most of the paddles – especially those in the $50+ category – are equally good, albeit they might be technically different in ways that won't affect the play of most beginners.

DON'T GET TOO CAUGHT up in all of the technicalities of paddle makeup when selecting your first paddle, but go with the one that feels right for you and that will give you the confidence to perform well. When choosing your first paddle, it is obviously wise to keep within your budget, but equally as important to think of things like grip, weight, and style of play, so that you can derive the most enjoyment and best experience when learning how to play pickleball.

. . .

THERE ARE LITERALLY thousands of paddles on the market, and most of them cost less than $100, which makes it extremely affordable to get involved in pickleball. There is not a huge difference in performance when buying any paddle for less than $80. With pickleball, you can experiment cheaply with all different types of paddles to find the one that works best for you, both in terms of play ability and also comfort. If you wanted to play today, you could go to your local Walmart, Dick's Sporting Goods, or tennis shop and buy a paddle and balls for under $50 total and go play for free at the nearest pickleball court, or even on a truncated tennis court if there are no pickleball specific courts in your area. Additionally, Amazon has dozens of pickleball paddle brands, with prices ranging from $10 to upwards of $200, but the most important criteria when buying your first paddle (other than cost) is selecting one that feels good to you.

What to Consider When Buying a Pickleball Paddle

Paddle Weight

THE FIRST THING TO look for when trying out different paddles is the weight of the paddle. The weight of pickleball paddles can vary greatly and affect your play style in many different ways. Paddles can range from 6 ounces on the light end all the way to more than double that weight at 14 ounces. It is definitely a personal preference as to which paddle weight feels the best to you, and the feeling of having a comfortable swing while having good mobility carrying the paddle is arguably the most important aspect of buying your first paddle. If you have friends or family who play pickleball, definitely think about trying out their paddles to get a feel for what will work best for you. If you aren't lucky enough to know someone who has a pickleball paddle for you to try before buying, consider going to a brick and mortar sporting goods store to try out different weight paddles. If you are unsure, a mid-weight paddle would probably be the best for you to start out with, just to be safe.

IF YOU ARE interested in different play styles for your first paddle, light and heavy paddles have different pros and cons. The lighter paddles give you more control in your shots and allow better maneuverability around the court. If you are a more athletic player who wants to run around and play singles more than doubles, a light paddle may be the best choice. You are going to be taking shots all over the court and running side to side, so control and being able to navigate to all areas of the court easily is important.

CONSIDER A HEAVIER PADDLE if you are a less active person who is taking up pickleball as more of a hobby rather than as a cardio workout or intense competition. Also, for doubles players, heavier paddles can be better as you generally play closer to the net in doubles and can generate a lot of power with a shorter swing. So the obvious cons of a heavier paddle are having less maneuverability and less control, but the cons of the lighter paddle are actually an increased risk of injury or soreness, when it seems like it would be the opposite. With the lighter paddles, you have to swing harder to generate the same amount of power as a heavier paddle with a lesser swing, so it increases the risk of tennis elbow or developing shoulder issues. The weight decision ultimately comes down to power vs. control in your play style and then personal preference regarding your comfort and confidence and the risk of injury.

Paddle Grip

Something that can be overlooked, but is arguably just as important as the weight of the paddle for the feel of the game and sense of control, is the grip. You want a grip that fits your hand but is not too small or too big, which can cause unnecessary strain on your wrist and elbow when playing. Believe it or not, the grip size actually has an effect on your play style as well. A smaller grip allows your wrist to move more freely and can increase the control of the ball for more spin and power. Having a smaller grip, however, can also allow too much movement, which can cause discomfort when swinging. A bigger grip will give you a more stable hit, which eases the tension your swing will put on your wrist and elbow. Make sure to not over-do it with your grip size, though, as a grip that is too large can put strain on your elbow. Most paddles that you will buy under $80 will not come with a premium grip, but you can buy grips to replace or add on to your paddle. These premium grips can actually absorb sweat and can help you get to your ideal grip size if you can't find a stock paddle that meets your needs for exact weight and grip size. To learn more about grip size, see "How to Find your Pickleball Paddle Grip Size" at hirdshotdrop.com.

Paddle Material

The other aspect to consider besides the grip, is the actual paddle material. As I mentioned earlier, there are many fancy words to describe the new technology and materials the manufacturers are putting into paddles these days.

WOOD: The first is a **wooden paddle,** which is really not a viable option for your first paddle if you have any ambition to become a decent pickleball player. These are the cheapest paddles in most cases and also on the heavier end of paddle weights. You probably won't see anyone on the pickleball courts anywhere (except maybe for children, or those who haven't done their homework) using a wooden paddle.

COMPOSITE: The next, and undoubtedly most popular material for pickleball paddles, is the **composite paddle.** They are in the middle range with respect to price, performance, and durability. Composites can be great for beginner pickleball players because they also come in a wide range of sizes, weights, and grips, so you can find the one that fits all of your needs.

GRAPHITE: The other option is the **graphite paddle,** which tends to be a little more expensive. These paddles are some of the lightest and give you the most control, but they are also strong and durable. Many consider graphite paddles the best-performing paddle, but they can also be too expensive for most people's budget for their first introductory paddle.

Paddle Size

. . .

Interestingly enough, there are no regulations on how wide or long your paddle can be; rather, the allowed size of the paddle is determined by the combination of both. Pickleball paddles cannot exceed 24 inches in a combination of the height plus the width. There are four main dimensions that pickleball paddles come in, but the combinations of sizes are ultimately endless as it gets down to as precise as an eighth of an inch with these measurements.

The standard paddle shape is 15 3/4" x 7 7/8", and this is widely considered to have been the first paddle size when the sport was invented. It is still one of the most common sizes sold and one of the most popular you will see out on the court on any given day. This is probably a good choice if you want to fit in and start with something that most people use instead of one of the more unique shapes that require different skill sets or techniques.

Another popular shape is what's known as the **wide body shape** at 16" x 8"; this paddle is good for beginner players and offers a wider paddle face to increase the contact area. If you are new to the game, this paddle will provide you with a smaller learning curve as it will be easier to pick up the sport and be more consistent until you are ready to move up to a more performance-based paddle shape.

The thin body **shape** is for those who want to get right into competitive games with their first paddle, as this is a lengthy 16 1/2" x 7 1/4". Many experts believe that the sweet spot to hit with this paddle is towards the top of the paddle, so the longer the paddle, the bigger that sweet spot will be. This is for more experienced, or pro players, and for your first paddle, it may not be advisable unless you expect to be competing with more experienced players right away and generally have a short learning curve for new sports.

Pickleball paddles get even longer with what they call the **blade paddle** at 17" x 6 7/8". These paddles require that your aim is on point, as they are also the narrowest paddles. The blade paddle actually gives you even more control on your shots, however, and many pros use this shape paddle to give them that extra edge in matches.

2. Ball

If you're new to pickleball, you may be wondering what kind of ball you should use. The three main types of pickleball balls are pressurized, plastic, and outdoor. Pressurized balls have a hard rubber or nylon core and a softer outer shell. This construction makes them ideal for indoor play as they bounce well on hard surfaces.

Plastic balls are made entirely of hard plastic and have a more textured surface than pressurized balls. These balls don't bounce as well as pressurized balls, but they are less likely to crack or shatter if they hit a hard surface. Outdoor pickleball balls are designed specifically for playing on outdoor courts. They have a textured surface to help them grip the pavement and a hollow core to resist wind gusts.

Regardless of what type of ball you use, make sure to keep an eye on it during play. Pickleballs can crack or break if they hit something too hard, so it's essential to inspect your ball regularly and replace it if necessary. With a bit of practice, you'll be hitting the pickleball like a pro in no time.

3. Net

PICKLEBALL NETS ARE MADE of nylon or polyester and are designed to be durable and easy to set up. When choosing a pickleball net, it is crucial to consider its size, material, and height. The net's regulation height is 34 inches for men and 36 inches for women. The net should also be tight so that the ball can bounce off of it easily.

THE NET USED in pickleball is similar to the net used in tennis but slightly smaller. The court size for pickleball is also smaller than a tennis court, so the net is designed to fit the smaller court size. Pickleball nets come in various materials, so choose one that is durable and easy to set up.

4. Shoes

YOU REALLY SHOULD PLAY pickleball with a pair of court shoes, specifically. They will provide you with some ankle and arch support, they have good grip on the ground, and they don't leave scuffs.

CHOOSING COMFORTABLE PICKLEBALL SHOES: This should be an easy one you would think. We have all bought tennis-style shoes at some point in our lives so what is the big deal about pickleball shoes? For me, nothing! I wear Wilson tennis shoes. They are not cheap. They cost $120 on Amazon, but they last a long time, are comfortable, and have a rubber sole that provides excellent traction.

BESIDES WILSON, K-Swiss, Head, New Balance, Adidas, and FILA are popular brands for pickleball players, but in truth, it doesn't really matter what brand of shoe you buy. It can get crazy if you try to choose a shoe based on what others have to say. There are some who distinguish between indoor and outdoor shoes. Outdoor shoes, they say, should have a rubber sole similar to tennis shoes for traction and grip on outdoor courts. Indoor pickleball shoes should have gummy rubber soles to maximize traction on basketball or gym floors. To me, this is nonsense, but what do I know? Go get yourself a pair of comfortable tennis-style sneakers. End of story!

ALSO, some places require court shoes in order to play on their courts.

5. **Other Materials**
    Athletic shorts
    Sweatpants
    Wicking apparel
    T-shirts
    Sneakers
    Sunglasses
    Hats
    Visors
    Sweatbands

Light jackets
Sweat shirts

Court Layout

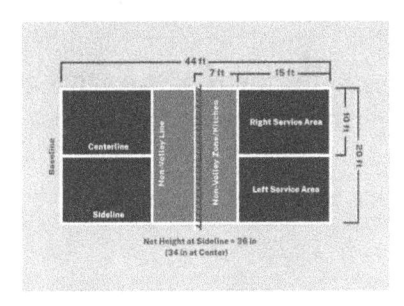

The key to enjoying pickleball is a well-laid-out court. A pickleball court is divided into different areas by lines, and each player is only allowed to stand in their respective areas.

PLAYING Area

THE PLAYING AREA is the main court where the game of pickleball is played. It is 20 feet wide by 44 feet long for indoor courts and 20 feet wide by 64 feet long for outdoor courts. The playing area is divided into two halves by a centerline, and each half is further divided into two quarters by a centerline. The sideline and baseline boundaries are also marked by lines.

NON-VOLLEY ZONE

. . .

This area also known as the "kitchen," is located near the net and extends seven feet on either side. Players cannot hit the ball into this zone while it is their turn to serve, and if they do, they give a point to the other side. The non-volley zone is marked by a line that runs perpendicular to the net and is seven feet from the edge of the court on either side. The non-volley zone is one of the many features that makes pickleball an exciting and challenging game for players of all ages.

Service Zone

The Pickleball Service Zone is the area of the court between the non-volley zone and baseline. The game's main objective is to score points by hitting the ball into your opponent's half of the court. To do this, players must stand inside the service zone when serving the ball. If the ball hits the ground in your opponent's half of the court, you will score a point.

Players cannot step on or over the lines when serving the ball. The ball must be hit with an underhand stroke. Each player can only serve from half of the service zone. The left side is for the player serving first, and the right side is for the player receiving the serve.

General Rules

1. **The Serve:** Players must serve the ball underhand and from behind the baseline. As in tennis, the ball must land in the diagonal service zone of the

other player to be considered a legal serve. If the ball hits the net on a serve, it is considered a let and is replayed.
2. **The Return:** The ball can be hit anywhere on the court, but it must clear the net. If the ball hits the net on a return, it is considered a let and is replayed.
3. **The Volley:** After the ball has bounced once, players can hit it before it bounces again. This is called a volley. Volleys can be hit anywhere on the court, but players cannot hit the ball into the non-volley zone. If the ball hits the ground in the non-volley zone, it is considered a fault, and the point is awarded to the other team.
4. **The Doubles Alley:** The alleys are the areas on either side of the court bordered by the sidelines and the service line. In doubles pickleball, players must stay within their respective alleys when serving or returning the ball. A player is only allowed to leave their alley when they are hitting a volley.
5. **Fault:** A fault is any time the ball does not land in the correct area or if a player steps on or over a line. When a fault is called, the point is awarded to the other team.
6. **Foot Fault:** A foot fault is called when a player is serving the ball steps on or over the baseline before hitting the ball. This results in a point for the other team.
7. **Dead Ball:** A dead ball is called when the ball hits an obstruction on the court, such as a player or a piece of equipment. The point is replayed.
8. **Do Not Disturb:** When a player is about to hit the ball, the other players must give them space and

be silent. This is so the player can focus on hitting the ball. The point is replayed if a player is disturbed while hitting the ball.
9. **Time-Outs:** Each team is allowed one 60-second time-out per game. Time-outs can be used to discuss strategy with your teammates or to take a break.
10. **Substitutions:** Substitutions can be made at any time, but players can only sub in for one player on their team.
11. **Non-Playing Coach:** A non-playing coach is allowed to advise their team from the sidelines, but they cannot interfere with the game.
12. **The Referee and the Line Judges:** The referee is responsible for making sure the game is played fairly and according to the rules. The line judges are responsible for making calls on whether the ball hits the lines. They can also make calls on whether a ball is in or out.

Fundamentals

Like any sport, there are certain fundamentals that you'll need to master to play your best game.

Services Sequence

ONE OF THE most crucial aspects of pickleball is service sequence. This simply refers to the order in which players serve. Typically, the player who scores last will serve first in the next game. However, if both players score on their serves, then the player who served first will serve again. This sequence continues until one player fails to score, at which point that player will lose the serve, and the other player will serve again.

Scoring

One of the best things about pickleball is how easy it is to learn how to score. The game is played to 11 points, with the winner being the first to reach two points ahead of their opponent (for example, if the score is 10-8, the next point would end the game). If the score reaches 10-10, the game goes to a tiebreaker. In a tiebreaker, the first player to reach seven points wins.

1. **Side-Out Scoring:** Side-out scoring is used in pickleball, meaning players can only score when they are serving. When a player loses their service, they will become the receiver, and their opponent will become the server. This guarantees that everyone has an equal chance of scoring.

2. **Advantage Scoring:** One of the unique features of pickleball is its scoring system, which allows players to earn points even when they are not serving. This is known as "advantage scoring." When one player has the advantage, the other player must continue to serve until they win a point. This system ensures that even when players are not serving, they still have a chance to score points. This adds excitement to the game and creates opportunities for come-from-behind victories.

. . .

3. **No-Ad Scoring:** No-Ad scoring is another option that can be used in pickleball. This system is similar to tennis, in which the first player to four points wins the game. No-Ad scoring can be used in games to 11 points, but the winner must be two points ahead of their opponent. However, this is an optional rule and is not typically used in general play.

Rules of Doubles Pickleball

In doubles pickleball, there are some slightly different rules that players need to be aware of. For example, when serving the ball, players must serve from behind the baseline and must alternate serves between themselves and their partner. In addition, players are not allowed to step on or over the baseline when returning the ball.

HERE ARE a few of the simple yet essential rules that players need to follow when playing doubles pickleball:

- ALTERNATE SERVES: Both players on a team must serve, and they must alternate serves between themselves. Players cannot double-fault, meaning they cannot serve two consecutive faults.

- NO STEPPING ON THE BASELINE: When returning the ball, players cannot step on or over the baseline. If a player steps on the baseline, it is considered a fault, and their opponents will be awarded the point.

. . .

- **SERVICE ZONE:** This is the area behind the baseline where players must stand when serving the ball. In doubles pickleball, each team has its service zone.

- **DOUBLES ALLEY:** The doubles alley is the area between the two service zones. This area is off-limits to both teams, and if a player steps into the doubles alley, it is considered a fault.

How to Do Exercise Properly

People begin to lose muscular mass as they become older. In actuality, beyond the age of 30, we drop 3%-5% every decade. Pickleball players may not think this is a big issue. After all, they don't require biceps to be pumped to properly cut out a Wiffle ball of their opponent's grasp. Less muscle, however, might result in increased frailty and decreased movement. It may also ultimately result in less time being spent in the courts; now, let's talk about the top strength training routines for keeping pickleball players active.

1. Plank

Your pelvis, stomach, hips, as well as lower back, are all trained with core movements. More powerful core muscles improve balance and stability. Strengthening the core plus upper body is aided by planks. This is excellent for pickleball because every time that you swing at a ball, you have to rotate the hips & upper body.

How to do the plank:

- Lie on your stomach on the ground.
- Place your hands exactly behind your shoulders with the palms towards the floor.
- Straighten your knees and thrust your torso up as if you were performing a pushup.
- Keep the bottom flat like such a table, your back upright, and the arms at the sides.
- Use the core to provide stability and to aid in maintaining proper form.
- Maintain the posture for 20–30 secs.
- To rest, get on your knees.
- Repeat the plank after a 60 to 90 second period of rest.
- Repeat four to five times, or as often as you possibly can.

2. Squat

While playing pickleball, you often squat and knelt to position yourself for a decent shot or even to grab for a ball. Your reaction time will improve, and overall stamina will increase as your thighs and legs gain strength.

Explanation:

- Stand with feet at about hip-width apart to shoulder-width away.
- Your toes should be slightly turned outward. Place your left side foot's toes at 10 o'clock on your right side foot's toes at 3 o'clock, picturing arms on the clock.
- Move your shoulders back, chest open, & spine neutral.
- Place your hands next to the chest in a prayer stance and place your heels downward flat.
- Drop yourself as if you were seated in an ethereal chair.
- Keep the chest firm and erect while bending your legs to descend as far as you can. Keep the thighs parallel to your knees at all times.
- Stay at the base level for a second.
- Put pressure on your feet to stand straight once again.
- Repeat.
- Do a set of eight to ten repetitions, pause for 60 to 90 seconds, and repeat.
- Attempt to complete 4 to 5 sets.

3. Lunge

When you twist, bend, and move sideways across the court while playing pickleball, strengthening your ankle and knee stability can help you avoid injury. Stamina may be increased by strengthening your legs, which have large muscles for the body.

PERFORMING LUNGES:

- Standing erect and firmly planted on your feet
- Lean forward and advance with 1 foot. Imagine it as 1.5 times your regular step.
- Drop your back knee more towards the floor while using your rear leg as support.
- The front knee should be parallel with the floor when you pause. Avoid extending your thigh beyond the knee.
- Pressing through the heel, raise yourself right back using your rear leg.
- Change legs.
- Continue 4-5 times, switching up each repetition.
- Do a second set after a 60 to 90 break.
- Plan on 4-5 sets.

MODIFICATION:
To implement a modification:

- Don't degrade yourself too badly. Only few inches would be helpful.
- Grabbing onto back of the chair while you drop yourself downward is another way to help keep yourself steady.
- Lower yourself simply & hold for a short period of time before you start rising and perform fewer repetitions if the continual ups and downs irritate you.
- At first, learning to do lunges might be challenging. You may gradually become better by using a seat or a wall.

4. Glute Bridge

Pickleball is a good sport for glute bridging because it helps you become more explosive, which increases the force of your shots also speeds up your response time. Glute bridges improve knee stability and strength, which may help avoid injuries.

. . .

How to do glute bridges:

- Your knees should be bent & pointing upward while you rest flat onto the ground with the soles of the feet onto the ground.
- To activate your abdominals and stomach, bring the belly button inwards.
- As you plant your feet firmly on the ground, raise your hips straight up in the air.
- Pinch your butt while pushing upward.
- For several seconds, keep your belly in the air until bringing your back to the floor.
- Repeat for 6 to 8 times.
- After a short pause, complete 4-5 sets.

5. Pushup

The pickleball game plus your life will both benefit greatly from having a very strong core. Pushups assist build upper body as well as arm strength. You can smash shots with greater force, bend and stretch more easily, and quicken your response time by strengthening the muscles in the back& stomach, which are part of your core.

. . .

PERFORMING PUSHUPS:

- Do a flat stomach laydown.
- Placing your hands with a tiny gap between them and the shoulders.
- With your arms and hands, lift the body up.
- Make a straight plane from the back to the butt & legs by straightening your arms.
- Except for your hands & toes, every part of the body must be elevated off ground.
- Keep your whole body under control as you stoop until the chest is almost parallel to the ground.
- At the base, pause for a moment, then lift yourself right back using your hands.
- As often as you want, repeat.
- After a short rest, repeat the whole set.

Do any of these or other workouts often if you find that your overall pickleball play isn't quite where you desire it to be or if you simply want to give it a little more power. You'll surprise your opponents.

How to Find and Choose a Pickleball Coach

So, you're at a stalemate in a pickleball match. Perhaps you feel as if you ought to be having more success than you currently are while playing certain competitors in the rec leagues. Maybe you even aspire of taking part in elite competitions. Alternatively, you may want to improve your game simply to increase your enjoyment of time spent on the courts. Whatever the reason, you've concluded that you could use an objective observer to point out where you're falling short and advise you on how to fix the problem.

IN THE PAST, it was far easier to get tennis instructors at places like high schools, country clubs, and public parks than it was to find pickleball coaches. Fortunately, finding a pickleball instructor to help you hone your skills is becoming less of a challenge as the sport grows in popularity. Is this person really qualified to be your coach? You may also ask, is this trainer the appropriate fit for you?

MORE INDIVIDUALS than ever are interested in becoming pickleball coaches in their community. A few amateurs may do wonders for your game, but many others (and even some professionals) might be unintentionally teaching you harmful techniques or habits.

KEEP in mind that not all great coaches were formerly great players and that not all great players became great coaches. Their inability to even imagine making a slam dunk is largely irrelevant in terms of whether or not someone can lead their group to the championship.

. . .

THE SAME IS true for coaching; someone's medal count or national fame is no guarantee that they'll be an excellent mentor. Here are a few things to look out for when selecting a pickleball coach;

1. *Qualifications and professional pickleball teaching certification.* Look for one of the standard certifications: IPTPA (International Pickleball Teaching Professional Association), PPR (Professional Pickleball Registry), or PCI (Pickleball Coaching International). A good pickleball coach should have the right set of qualifications and certifications that reflect his or her skill set successfully. Think of these as the guarantee – a seal of authenticity – that the instructor has learned the necessary information and has the appropriate experience to teach the game successfully to others. These teacher-training programs cover various subjects, including (a) the fundamentals of the game, (b) how to communicate with students, (c) how to monitor students' progress, and (d) how to plan lessons and clinics. No matter what, as mentioned earlier, a good pickleball coach must have the right certifications before you consider training with that person.

2. *Excellent communication skills.* The way a coach communicates with the students can make all the difference between success and failure. A pickleball coach must be able to communicate in a clear, transparent manner. Suppose you are learning quickly what the coach is teaching. The coach should compliment you. Conversely, if you are not learning the skills being taught, the coach should have the confidence to critique you in an understanding fashion. But it works both ways; you should also feel comfortable discussing your

progress, or lack of progress, and be able to voice whatever concerns or questions you may have without any hesitation.

3. *Recommendations from others who have taken lessons or clinics.* It is always a good idea to speak to some of the coach's students to find out what they have to say about the coach. References and testimonials are very important. Although not a guarantee, if others have had a good experience with the coach, it means that there is a good chance you will too. Also consider how long the coach has been teaching. Generally speaking, look for a coach who has been teaching for a few years rather than someone who is just starting out. This shouldn't be an iron-clad rule because certainly, there could be teachers who have just started who are very good, but it is generally a good idea to favor the more experienced coach.

4. *The ability to structure lessons and monitor progress.* Unfortunately, it is difficult to determine whether or not a coach has these particular qualities until you have started taking lessons. What you are looking for is a coach who has a game plan (so to speak). Hopefully, the coach has a structured way of teaching fundamentals and knows when to move onto more advanced skill sets that will enable you to become a better player. The coach should be able to monitor your progress so he or she knows what to teach and when to teach it. The coach should also be able to provide you with the necessary feedback for you to continue improving in the sport.

5. *The level of the coach's pickleball playing ability.* A good pickleball coach can only teach what he or she knows. However,

keep in mind that a good pickleball instructor is not necessarily the best pickleball player on the planet. There are plenty of examples of professional sports coaches who never excelled at the sport they were coaching, but equally, there is a long list of elite athletes who failed as professional coaches. Being an elite professional will not make someone a better teacher than a highly competent amateur player, but a high level of knowledge and skill is still necessary, otherwise, how can those skills be passed on? A good teacher can help to improve higher-level skills in others that are beyond their own athletic ability.

6. *Patience and adaptability to different types of students.* I know it's hard to tell about a coach's character before you have started taking lessons, but you should be able to at least get a feel for it during an initial conversation while trying to make up your mind as to whether or not you want to take lessons with this person. A good coach should also be able to develop a program specifically for you, if it's a private lesson, and be willing to alter it once he or she sees how you progress. A lesson plan that works for one student doesn't always work for other students, so the coach needs to be flexible with his or her plan for you. A good coach should be able to adapt his or her teaching style not only to your level of ability but also to your personality.

7. *Ability to motivate students.* This is so important. A good teacher – a good coach – should be able to motivate you not only to play better, but, just as important, to *want* to play better. A coach's style, his or her teaching style, should include drills that are engaging, fun, and exciting in order to keep you motivated. A good coach can push you to improve

and help build your confidence, or regain your confidence when times are difficult and you might be struggling with a particular shot or skill. It's the coach's job to keep you motivated at all times.

I HOPE I'm not scaring you off with this long list of must-have teacher qualifications. What matters most is that a coach has a love and passion not only for the game of pickleball but, just as important, a love for teaching. Moreover, a coach must be able to communicate that passion, and their technical knowledge of the sport, to the students clearly and efficiently, so that they can learn to become better pickleball players. A good pickleball coach will keep students motivated through the journey of learning new skills, practicing, and improving their game.

IT'S NOT unusual to start with one coach and then realize he or she is not right for you, or that you need a different coach in order to progress further.

BE VERY careful about who you accept pickleball advice or coaching from.

THERE ARE MANY, many well-meaning individuals out there trying to be helpful or who like to share tidbits with others. However, much of this well-meaning advice should be taken with a grain of salt. Why? In my experience, most of this advice is simply regurgitated information from another source, which oftentimes is outdated or simply poor information.

. . .

LET ME ASK YOU THIS – would you take golf lessons or advice from a 30 handicap with no golf teaching experience? How about from a scratch golfer with no teaching experience? Or would you rather take golf advice from a seasoned golf professional who was/is a very strong player and has had years of experience studying best practices of various ages and ability levels, who learned from peers, has experience teaching and honing his/her skill sets, who learned from some of the other best teachers in the industry, and who had a great mentor? The answer should be obvious. Too often, pickleball players don't take this type of thinking into consideration. I think that's unfortunate.

IN MY OPINION, there are far too many unqualified or underqualified individuals giving advice on the pickleball court or, worse, trying to teach lessons for money (sometimes lots and lots of it).

THREE EXAMPLES of these individuals are as follows:

- HIGH-LEVEL PLAYERS who have playing talent but possess little to no teaching background. Unsuspecting folks too often pay outrageous amounts of money for these lessons. If you wanna pay a boatload for a selfie, feel free. But please don't equate playing ability with teaching ability. They are not even close to the same thing. Do not assume because someone is a great player that they can teach well.

. . .

- PLAYERS WITH A TENNIS playing background who think they can teach pickleball because they know a bit about playing tennis. Pickleball is not tennis, nor is it small tennis. While there are some similarities and transferable skills, pickleball is a different game.

- INDIVIDUALS with some tennis teaching experience who assume they can teach pickleball because they have taught tennis in the past. While this person MAY be a good pickleball teacher, it is not a guarantee until time proves it to be so. Again, pickleball is not like mini tennis. The differences are greater than the similarities. For what it's worth, I would take this person above either of the aforementioned individuals. I mean, at least they have some experience teaching a racquet sport.

Now, I'm not suggesting all tips given on the court are bad or that individuals giving advice or lessons are duping good people out of money on purpose. What I am doing is suggesting to good people who want to learn to do some research and not accept every piece of advice as if it's good advice. There is a ton of bad advice floating around out there. Make sure you are getting advice from a worthy source.

IF YOU'RE GIVING advice or wanting to give lessons, I'm begging you! Please, make sure you know what you're talking about or else maybe keep your thoughts to yourself. Don't continue to spread bad or unhelpful information, because there is enough to go around already.

. . .

If you're RECEIVING ADVICE, please filter it the best you can. Yes, it can be very challenging to separate the wheat from the chaff, but I recommend you only listen to advice from well qualified teachers of the game who really know what they're talking about and aren't simply repeating what they may have heard from someone on a YouTube video.

BE VERY careful about who you get your pickleball advice from!

How to Find a Certified Pickleball Coach

THE BEST WAY TO find a good, professional pickleball teacher is to ask others who have taken lessons for a recommendation. If you go to the park or recreation center, you can ask if anyone has taken lessons and get names. Sometimes you might even see a lesson or clinic in progress, and of course, you can easily ask the instructor for a business card.

MANY TENNIS CENTERS are now offering private lessons and clinics in pickleball. Also, indoor and outdoor facilities dedicated exclusively to pickleball are springing up all over the world; no doubt you can find certified instructors at these venues.

YOU COULD JOIN a Facebook group such as Pickleball Instructor Forum or Pickleball for Beginners. Most likely, there are also Facebook groups in your area dedicated to pickleball. In southeastern Florida, for example, there are at least a dozen pickleball Facebook groups.

OTHER OPTIONS INCLUDE:

- Pickleball Teachers Network
- Professional Pickleball Registry
- International Pickleball Teaching Professional Association
- Global Pickleball Network
- Meetup Groups (there are dozens of Meetup groups throughout the world dedicated to pickleball, including mine)
- Google "pickleball private lessons near me".

How to Best Select between Private and Clinic Pickleball Sessions

PRIVATE PICKLEBALL SESSIONS

ONE-ON-ONE TIME IS INCLUDED in the private pickleball sessions.

WHAT YOU'LL DISCOVER **from this experience**

- advanced poaching
- building weapons
- advanced drilling

- misdirection & fakes
- why you hit the strikes you hit
- point breakdown
- proceeding to the kitchen
- court positioning
- footwork and paddle position
- erne's, atp's and defending them
- reading the opponent
- slices, drives & blocks
- tournament prep
- hiding weaknesses & utilizing strengths
- resets &defense
- turning defense towards offense
- advanced kitchen plan
- panic mode
- mental game
- team strategy
- technique & stroke production
- staying energetic off the ball
- controlling point
- space & time

What will impress you about them

- Individualized training with a guide
- In-depth planning and competitive analysis
- Unique & inventive exercises & games
- Compete with and against experienced players.
- Fun & laughter

Clinic Pickleball Sessions

PARTICIPATING in pickleball clinics is an excellent method to enhance one's skills. Pickleball clinics are geared at gamers of all skill levels, from beginners to intermediates, who want to focus on improving a particular facet of the game. The clinics go for a total of 90 mins, with 60 mins devoted to teaching and the remaining 30 minutes open for free play. The number of people that may participate in a clinic is capped at eight so that everyone has a fantastic time. A payment in advance is necessary.

LEARN about Pickleball clinics

HERE IS what you should expect:

1. An exposure to Pickleball - Become an expert on the sport that others are talking about.

- How to make note of the score
- Game overview
- Basic shot approaches
- Fundamentals of the court system
- The service and receiving of the ball

2. Blocking - Are you sick and tired of being hit by bangers? Make use of the authority they possess against them.

- Tips for defeating bangers
- The significance of maintaining paddle up
- Accelerating after a slam

- How to transition from defense to offense in a quick
- Blocking the point to start again

3. Strategy & court positioning - collaborate to grow better.

- Find out your team's qualities and weaknesses.
- Analyze the ball's flight.
- Moving together

4. Lobbing and Defending Lob - Guard against the terrible lob.

- a good gait and court knowledge
- Knowing when to lob is important.

5. Dinking 101 - Gain court management skills while having a fun.

- possess court position
- Volley Dinks
- Manage the game
- Footwork
- Conduct the pickleball dance as a partner.

6. Dinking 201 - Have you dinked before? Time to start acting aggressively now.

- How to dink the ball while keeping it low
- Using good footwork will position you for a fantastic dink.
- When to take the next shot, when to do it

7. Double Strategy or Serving - Come practice the Jedi Techniques as you study them.

- middle forehand with authority
- Stacking
- How to strike the less-skilled opponent
- Deep serves: If your serve is not received, you cannot score.
- Who has the dreaded middle?
- Recognizing your position on the court
- recognizing patterns

8. Exercises to improve your game - Fantastic drills to improve your game.

- Singles on a half court
- Returns & Serves Deep
- Drills for dinking
- Blocking Exercise

9. Pushing the backhand - Learn backhand shot methods while having some fun and becoming better.

- The ideal location to score big
- court approval
- Backhand exercises
- becoming more at ease using your backhand

10. When and how to attack - Having reached the kitchen barrier, it's time to decide when to launch an attack.

- How to strike a ball
- Using touch above power

- What areas of the court are ideal for attacks?

11. **Poaching - Determine the ideal moment to occupy the court.**

    - Stacking
    - Court placement
    - Preserving the center with forehands

12. **Poaching or Stacking - Maintain the proper posture of the stronger partner.**

    - Court placement
    - escaping difficult circumstances, mostly on court
    - Maintain the middle with the better forehand.
    - jumping kitchen line

13. **Getting ready for the tournament - Prepare both physically and emotionally.**

    - Prepare you as well as your partner for victory.
    - Despite difficulties, maintain your calmness

14. **3rd goal skills and drills - Improve your ability to go to the net.**

    - The third shot is what?
    - In what ways does this help my game?
    - allowing you sufficient time to reach the kitchen
    - 3rd shot, contact backhand.
    - 3rd shot with force and poach

15. **Improving your serve: Improve your consistency and ace catching.**

- Learn the value of serving at a deep level and how to achieve it.
- The ideal starting points to serve from
- Where to direct the ball to make it harder for opponents

16. **When to appropriately strike the ball in volleyball before it returns for the very first time.**

- volley dinking
- Blocks
- Put aside shots

Beginner Clinic

Study the foundations and principles. Ideal for anyone who has never played before.

Advanced Learner Clinic

Ideal for individuals who have completed all three Beginner Pickleball Clinic courses. Keeping score is a need.

Intermediate Clinic

. . .

EXPAND on the knowledge gained during the Enhanced Beginners Clinic. Beneficial for individuals with ratings up to 3.5.

PICKLEBALL IS an excellent game for all ages and skill levels. Whether you are just starting or have been playing for years, the information in this chapter will help you improve your game.

3
GETTING STARTED

Now that we've explored the roots of pickleball and its evolution into the game we know today, let's take a look at how to get started playing. While the game may seem simple at first, many strategies are involved in becoming a pickleball champion. There are a few basic strokes you'll need to master, along with some know-how on winning and keeping the rally going.

THIS CHAPTER WILL COVER the pickleball serve, the three main strokes (forehand, backhand, and volleying), and some tips on winning and extending the rally. By the end of this chapter, you'll be well on your way to playing pickleball like a pro!

Understanding the Pickleball Serve

For some reason, many otherwise great players struggle with the serve. Once their confidence is shaken, the struggle worsens. I think if you follow the suggestions below, you can end any struggles you may have.

Serving is a Privilege, Make the Most of It

Your team can score points only when serving. Don't blow your serve. Beginning in 2021, there are no "let" serves or do-overs. If your serve touches the net then somehow lands in the correct section of the opponents' court, it's good and game on. It may have lost some of its spirit by brushing the top of the net, but it's playable. But, if your serve lands in the opponents' kitchen area or out of bounds, you just lost your team's chance to earn a point. Big mistake.

The same player keeps serving as long as his team keeps winning points. The server alternates serving from the right side and the left side of the court.

Develop a Pre-Serve Routine

All great golfers and tennis players have a pre-shot routine where they set up for success and for a smooth and continuous journey toward making the strike. If you watch the professional tennis players on the Tennis Channel you will see that the pre-serve routine is extremely consistent from serve to serve. The following is a suggested routine.

Set your feet. I use a stance that is roughly square to my opponent. However, many top players use other variations.

Focus and visualize the ball flight path.

Bounce the ball a few times. Most tennis players do this.

Call the score, ensure your opponent is ready, and spot your target, for example, dead center of the service box. Talking or calling the score while serving can distract you and cause faults.

While holding the ball against the center of the paddle, visualize a ball flight path that provides a very generous clearance above the net. Rotate your wrist to the right (for a right-handed player) to enable having the paddle face aimed at (square to) the target flight path.

Draw the paddle back while attempting to keep the face from shifting left or right of the target.

Hold the ball from above and drop it as you swing the paddle forward, trying to keep the paddle face always pointing to the ball flight path.

Once you serve, make sure you quickly get back into ready position behind the baseline.

Like the tennis pros, try to avoid any hesitations or variance. If any interruption occurs, go back to Step 2 above. Usually when I have a service fault, I realize that I was not disciplined in following the routine.

MANY PLAYERS USE a serve where they step across the baseline when serving. It is perfectly okay to step into this shot. If you do this, you should get back behind the baseline in time to judge the return of serve shot, which could come to you very deep. Neither member of the serving team should be inside the baseline until after the return of serve shot has been evaluated. It's nearly impossible to hit a great third shot if you are retreating while trying to hit it. It's much easier to travel into the court than to travel out.

SOME OF THE service swing comes from the weight shift toward the lead foot or the stepping out, some of the movement comes from upper torso rotation, and some comes from the shoulder. The arm moves like a pendulum from the shoulder. The movement is very similar to a straight bowling ball release.

I SEE many social players use a very quick swatting action that uses wrist action. Though many folks are successful with this, I would never recommend it. Instead, I think it's best to minimize paddle face rotation and curving at the moment of impact. This can be achieved by reducing wrist and elbow action and letting the swing come from the torso and shoulder.

TO SOME EXTENT, you can "groove in" your routine in your home, even if you have no practice wall. Just go through the steps and pretend to make a strike. If you have access to a gymnasium or tennis practice wall, you can practice your serve using a wall. You can use easy-to-remove painter's tape to mark the top of an imaginary net and a target spot. Otherwise you can practice on an empty pickleball court.

Serving Territory

To serve, when you strike the ball both feet must be behind the baseline and in an area represented by an imaginary extension of the sidelines and the centerline of your court.

It's okay if your feet cross the baseline with your follow through after you connect with the ball. One more thing: at least one foot must be on the ground when you connect with the ball – that means no "Air Jordan."

Once you execute the traditional or drop serve correctly from your court – half the battle – it must clear the net and land in the diagonal quadrant of your opponents' court beyond their kitchen line.

If the ball lands in the opponents' kitchen or touches the kitchen line it is short and a fault. If it lands beyond the baseline or outside the center or sideline, you messed up.

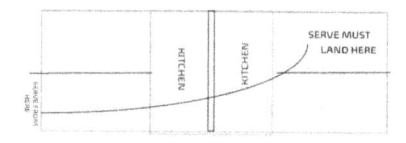

Serving Styles

Serves are the first opportunity to score in pickleball, and there are a few different ways to do it. All serves must be underhand and hit diagonally into the opposite court. The server can stand anywhere behind the baseline but must serve from the same courtside for the entire game.

1. The Backhand Serve

The backhand keeps your opponent off-balance and allows you to put more spin on the ball. To execute a backhand serve, start by positioning yourself at the back of the court. Stand with your feet shoulder-width apart and your weight on your back foot. Then, toss the ball up into the air and hit it with your paddle, using an underhanded motion.

Ensure to follow through with your stroke and aim for the center of your opponent's court. The key to a successful backhand serve to keep your paddle low and hit the ball at waist level. This allows you to have more control over the ball and keep it on the court. The backhand serves as a great option for beginners, as it is relatively easy to master.

2. The Forehand Serve

. . .

ONE OF THE most common serves in pickleball is the forehand serve. To execute a forehand serve, stand facing the front of the court with your feet shoulder-width apart. Bend your knees and bring the paddle back behind you, then snap your wrist to hit the ball diagonally into the opposite court.

THE FOREHAND SERVES as one of the most important strokes in pickleball. Unlike the backhand serve, which an opponent can easily return, the forehand serve is much more difficult to defend. As a result, it can be a very effective weapon, particularly when used to surprise an opponent who is expecting a backhand.

THE KEY to a successful forehand serve to keep your wrist firm and hit the ball with the sweet spot of your paddle. This will generate a lot of power and spin, making it difficult for your opponent to return the shot. With a little practice, you'll be able to master the forehand serve and use it to take your game to the next level.

3. The Power Serve

THE POWER SERVE is one of the most important strokes in pickleball. A properly executed power can help you gain an early advantage in the game and put your opponent on the defensive. While there are various ways to execute a power serve, the most key crucial factor is generating enough spin to keep the ball low over the net. This can be accomplished by using a wrist snap and keeping your arms parallel to the ground as you make contact with the ball.

. . .

Another tip is to aim for the corners of the court, giving your opponent less time to react. The key to a successful power serve is to practice, practice, practice. The more you serve, the more comfortable you'll become with the stroke, and the more likely you are to execute it flawlessly in a game situation. You'll get closer to perfecting your power serve with every game.

4. The High Soft Serve

Whether you're a beginner or a seasoned pro, everyone can agree that the high soft serve is one of the essential shots in pickleball. Not only does it help to keep your opponent on their toes, but it also allows you to control the game and dictate the pace. To execute a successful high soft serve, keep the ball low and slow. This way, your opponent will have difficulty getting under the ball and will be forced to lob it back high, giving you an easy winner.

The high serve is one of the most challenging strokes in pickleball, but it can be very effective when done correctly.

To start:

Stand at the back of the court and toss the ball up into the air.

. . .

SWING your paddle around your body and hit the ball with an upward motion.

FOLLOW through with your stroke and hit the ball at waist level. This will ensure that the ball stays low and doesn't go out of bounds.

WITH A BIT OF PRACTICE, you'll be hitting high soft serves like a pro in no time.

5. The Angled Serve

The angled serve in pickleball is a powerful weapon that can help you win points. When executed correctly, it can send the ball sailing past your opponents and into the corner of the court. But what exactly is an angled serve? How do you execute it properly?

AN ANGLED serve is a service that is hit with an angle rather than straight on. You can do this by holding your paddle at an angle when hitting the ball or by using a power spin. When hit correctly, an angled serve will travel across the court at a sharp angle, making it difficult for your opponents to return.

TO EXECUTE AN ANGLED SERVE, start by positioning yourself at the baseline on one side of the court. Then, hold your paddle out in front of you and slightly to the side. When you are ready, swing your paddle up and make contact with the ball at an angle. Be sure to put some spin on the ball to make it zig-zag across the court.

A Good Way to Learn How to Serve

A GOOD WAY TO minimize failure and immediately build confidence with serving is as follows. Instead of standing behind the baseline, stand very close to the net. See Figure 4-5. You might think this is so easy that it's ridiculous. However, I urge you to follow the system.

USE your complete pre-shot routine for every serve. Your aim point should be dead center of the service box. The ball flight path should clear the net by at least two feet. This gives you enough leeway for error.

EXECUTE the serve and note the landing spot.

REPEAT this until the ball is consistently landing in the middle of the box. Once you can get 10 in a row into the center of the box, move back a couple of feet.

REPEAT the above until you can get 10 in a row into the center of the box, then move back a couple of feet.

DO NOT JUST HIT the ball in the general direction of the service box. Instead, choose an exact target, visualize the exact trajectory you desire, and think about having the paddle face push the ball along the trajectory path.

. . .

You can also use a practice wall to develop your serving skill. Again, start close to ensure success, and then work further away.

For folks who are developing their skill my advice is this: focus on reliability. Your game will not be handicapped if you can consistently hit serves that land near the center of the box. Again, even at the very highest skill levels of pickleball, all that is necessary is a serve that does not fault and that can get about halfway back in the box. So, for developing players, I recommend aiming for the middle of the box and allowing at least several feet of clearance above the net.

Many pickleball teachers advise their students to practice serving deep or to backhands. My concern with this is that most attempts to hit targets away from the center of the box result in increased faults. In my opinion, of all the areas to work on in pickleball, working on getting a serve to land deeper than the center of the box should be low on the list.

The next time you go out to play, before each serve, spot the target (dead center of the box), and try to hit this target. Keep some mental notes on how well you did. I think you will find that hitting a target is more difficult than you think it is.

On your next outing, set a goal to have zero service faults. Count any faults that occur. Coach Mo drives the philosophy that you should not fault with your serve more than once per month.

OVER YOUR NEXT SEVERAL OUTINGS, develop your serving routine. It should always involve spotting the target and visualizing the ball flight, which should allow a generous clearance of the net and a wide margin for error.

The Art of Volleying in Pickleball

The game of pickleball is a fun and challenging sport that is growing in popularity all over the world. One of the key skills that players need to master is volleying. Volleying is when you hit the ball before it bounces on your side of the court. This can be a difficult shot to make, but when done correctly, it can give you a lot of control over the game.

THERE ARE a few things to remember when volleying. First, you want to make sure that you hit the ball in the center of your paddle. This will give you the most control over the shot. Second, you want to make sure that you keep your paddle low, close to the ground. This will help you keep the ball low, which is strategic in pickleball.

FINALLY, you want to ensure that you follow through with your shot. This will help you generate more power and spin on the ball. If you can master these three things, you will be well on your way to becoming a great pickleball player.

Footwork

. . .

Volleying is a vital skill in pickleball, and proper footwork is essential for executing a perfect volley. Here are some tips to help you get the most out of your footwork:

· Start by positioning yourself so that you're perpendicular to the ball's direction. This will give you the most power and control over your shot.

· As the ball comes towards you, take a small step towards it to meet the ball in the center of your paddle.

· Keep your weight balanced as you make contact with the ball. You don't want to be too far forward or back, as this will affect the power and accuracy of your shot.

· Finally, follow through with your stroke and end up in a ready position so that you can react to your opponent's next shot.

With these tips in mind, you'll be volleying like a pro in no time!

Positioning

. . .

One of the most important things to keep in mind when volleying is positioning. You want to make sure that you are positioned correctly to accurately hit the ball. Here are some tips to help you get the most out of your positioning:

• Stand with your feet shoulder-width apart and your weight evenly distributed. This will give you a strong base to work from.

• Bend your knees slightly and keep your racket arm ready. This will help you stay agile and ready to react to the ball.

• When you see the ball coming, step towards it and swing your racket through the ball. This will help you hit the ball in the center of your paddle.

• Follow through with your swing and end up in the same position as you started in.

When you are positioned correctly, you will have more power and control over your shot. Keep these tips in mind the next time you are volleying to make sure that you hit the ball perfectly.

Returning Smashes with Authority

. . .

ONE OF THE most challenging shots to return in pickleball is the smash. Smashes are powerful shots hit with a lot of spins. They can be difficult to return, but with these tips, you'll be able to return them with ease:

· THE FIRST THING you want to do is get in a low position. This will help you stay balanced and ready to react to the ball.

· NEXT, hit the ball in the center of your paddle. This will give you the most control over the ball.

· DON'T BE afraid to put a little extra spin on the ball. This will help you keep it in play and make it more difficult for your opponent to return.

· KEEP your eye on the ball at all times. This may seem like an obvious one, but it can be easy to lose track of the ball when it's coming at you so fast.

· FINALLY, follow through with your shot and end up in a ready position. This will help you stay agile and be prepared for your opponent's next shot.

WITH THESE SIMPLE TIPS, you'll not only dish out fantastic smashes but also return any smash that comes your way.

The Rally and Fault

When playing pickleball, there are two main ways to score points - the rally and the fault. The rally is when both players can keep the ball in play without making any mistakes. The player who then makes a mistake is said to have committed a fault. For a player to win a point, they must either win the rally or force their opponent to make a fault.

THERE ARE a few different types of faults that can be made in pickleball. The most common type is when the player hits the ball out of bounds. This can happen if the player hits the ball too high, too low, or too wide. Other faults include hitting the ball into the net, double-hitting the ball, or taking too long to hit the ball. If a player commits any of these faults, their opponent will be awarded a point.

WHILE SCORING POINTS is important in pickleball, it's also important to avoid making mistakes. This is because every time a player makes a fault, their opponent is allowed to score an easy point. As such, it's often said that the best offense is a good defense - by avoiding making mistakes, you can put your opponent in a position where they are more likely to make one.

Different Shots in Pickleball

One of the things that makes pickleball so enjoyable is the variety of shots that can be played. For example, players can choose to hit the ball with topspin or backspin, and they can also vary the amount of power they put into their shots. Additionally, players can place the ball anywhere on the court, making it possible to create all sorts of different angles and trajectories.

THE VAST ARRAY of shot possibilities is one of the things that makes pickleball such an addictive game. Whether playing competitively or just for fun, you'll never get bored of hitting the pickleball around. Here are some of the different types of shots that can be played in pickleball:

DINK Shots

A DINK IS A SOFT, short shot that goes over the net and lands in your opponents' kitchen. They will have to bend low to return it. A dinking contest is the meat of many points.

THE WHOLE IDEA **behind the dink is to "strike" the ball so it drops into the opponents'** NVZ AREA. You do not hit it over the net! **You push it over the net.** This is a huge difference in shot approach. Players who hit the ball over the net attempting to dink usually hit dinks that result in unforced errors or dinks that are very attackable. Players who hit their dinks usually take a back swing of 2' or more and this places far too much paddle power into the ball when you are only trying to hit the ball 5'-8'. A "straight-on-dink" has any where from 8'-14' to travel. A ball hit with a modified forehand or backhand back swing is going to be elevated over the net in an arc that is very attackable and probably will not drop into the opponents' NVZ. The solution is to push the ball back over the net. To push the ball with your forehand move/reach your paddle forward and in a "still" or stopped paddle position with the paddle head pointing to the ground, push the paddle getting as close to the ball as possible through the ball with about a 6" to 12" follow through. There is no wrist movement in the dink shot. Your wrist is locked as you push the paddle forward. The paddle as it moves forward will automatically lift the ball with enough height to clear the net.

THE BALL SHOULD GO over the net and drop into the opposite NVZ. If you need an "aiming spot" try and hit the dink 1'-2' over the net so it drops within 1'-3' from the net on the opponents' side. This ball cannot be hit aggressively.

PLEASE NOTE: THE "STRAIGHT AHEAD DINK" requires no back swing to fall into the 8'-14' space/distance. However, if you dink the diagonal line connecting the two opposite diagonal corners of your kitchen and the opponents' kitchen, the distance is almost 24'5" and using a forehand or backhand 2'+ back swing is useful in having the ball travel that distance. The very top players in dinking these greater distances (up to 24') will "open" their paddle at 45 degrees and push through the ball allowing the 45 degree paddle angle to elevate and drop the ball onto the other side of the net into opponents' NVZ. It is not a slice but a push with an open faced paddle. The paddle travels in a straight path through the ball. It does not travel in a high to low swing which is a slice swing. That swing goes into the net. The very top players short-hop the ball or half-volley it. Catching the dink coming to you on the "short-hop" puts a little backspin on the ball and allows a little more directional control. It is, however, more difficult to accurately control the distance the ball travels. If you are dinking straight across from you and short hop the ball you run a high risk of the ball popping up in the air and getting attacked by your opponents. Short-hopping the ball to dink diagonally has a much better margin-of-error as diagonally the ball stays/lands closer to the net and is not attackable. You can never over practice the dink shot! A great way to practice the dink shot is to play the dink game. This can be done as you are warming-up for your regular "club play". You play it as a regular game but the balls all have to be dinks or "dink volleys" and land into the opponents' NVZ. The server can either bounce the ball and serve it or hit a "regular" serve. All scoring and rotations are the same as a regular pickleball game. Do not underestimate the incredible benefits of this practice game.

Groundstroke

A GROUNDSTROKE IS a shot you hit after the ball has bounced. A volley is a shot you hit before it bounces.

A PASSING SHOT is like a line drive in baseball. It is an offensive shot that moves fast and in a straight line with no arc. It can be used to keep your opponent away from the net near the back of his court, a good place to stick him.

A LOB SHOT travels in a high arc over your opponent's head and lands near her baseline. She will have to turn around to try for it, or just let it go and hope it is long.

LOBS CAN BE A "RAINBOW" in your game but they usually result in a "downpour" of unforced errors. Three things can happen when you lob: (1) The lob can be hit too long and it goes out; (2) The lob can be hit too short and gets attacked by your opponents; and (3) The lob can be that "perfect" rainbow arc and fall onto the court non-returnable by your opponents. This "perfect" rainbow lob once achieved becomes the impetus for the next 20 lobs that fall into the other two classes of being too short and attacked by your opponent or too long and appreciated by your opponents. Just because there are three things that can happen to a lob does not mean you'll be successful 33% of the time. The vast majority of lobs are too long or too short. The "good" or "perfect" lob is seldom successful on the pickleball court. The very elite/top pickleball players will likely skip over this section as they do not lob essentially at all. Why? It's because they are younger, still in their athletic prime, and possess overheads that remind the players on the other side of the net why they shouldn't have lobbed. As we get older we still cover the same amount of court but it takes us longer to cover it. Our athletic "prime" is behind us.

WE RUN SLOWER and our reflexes diminish. The saving grace is knowing today's elite players will join our much larger group "tomorrow". In light of the fact that the vast majority of us realize the lob can be an effective weapon in our arsenal, we need to spend time examining the lob and the various aspects of its use and application. Just as there are offensive and defensive overheads there are, also, offensive and defensive lobs. There are so many factors and elements involved in "lobbing" successfully that the actual execution of the shot is very difficult and high risk in nature. Since two of the three things that can happen to lobs are not conducive to winning, most people don't even try to put this shot in their game. Even if you fall into this group, understanding the lob in all of its intricacies may help you better defend against it.

Overhead Shot

An overhead shot is one a player reaches high to hit. It is usually hit with a downward stroke and results in a slam the opponent will have trouble returning.

Overheads actually fall into the volley category since you are hitting a ball that hasn't bounced. It's very unlikely a ball/lob would be hit high enough that if allowed to bounce it would bounce high enough to become a "legitimate" overhead. Most overheads occur as a result of the opponents' lob strategies. In addition most lobs are offensive in nature and the shortness of the court limits the height of the lob. Defensive lobs can be hit as high as your opponent is able to hit it. A 20 foot high defensive lob allowed to bounce will bounce up roughly 8'8" which is high enough for an offensive overhead swing. This loses the volley status being allowed to bounce, but it's still an overhead swing or shot.

Important Point! There are probably more unforced errors hit from overheads than any other shot in pickleball.

Not only is the shot difficult to hit well under "perfect conditions", once you calculate in the extenuating circumstances of sun, wind, and the mental "gymnastics" that occur during preparation for the overhead, the overhead can become a really difficult shot to execute. A very common mistake made by pickleball players at all levels of play is assuming that any ball hit in the eight feet or higher range should be attacked in an "end the point" swing. Overheads fall into two categories: (1) Offensive, and; (2) Defensive. You must be able to immediately classify the overhead required as offensive or defensive. Your standing position on the court and the height and depth of the ball should lead to immediate recognition of your overhead as offensive or defensive.

OVERHEAD "RULE OF THUMB" – If the ball coming to your side is dropping in front of you or directly over your head it's an offensive overhead.

IF THE BALL is behind you and you don't have time to get set under the ball, then it's clearly a defensive overhead.

LOB SHOTS

LOB SHOTS ARE another important shot in pickleball. They are used when your opponent is at the net, and you are at the back of the court. A lob shot is a high arching shot that clears the net and lands just behind the baseline. When executed properly, a lob shot will give your opponent no chance of returning the ball.

TO HIT A LOB SHOT, you will need to use an underhand stroke. Begin by positioning yourself at the back of the court and your opponent at the net. When the ball is hit, let it bounce once before hitting it up into the air. Use an underhand stroke to hit the ball with a high arch. The ball should clear the net and land just behind the baseline.

Drop Shot

A DROP SHOT is a soft shot that lands just over the net, causing it to drop sharply and making it difficult for your opponent to return. Drop shots are often used as a defensive strategy since they allow you to keep your opponent near the back of the court, where they are less likely to score. However, they can also be used as an offensive strategy, forcing your opponent to move forward and open up the court for a possible winner. Regardless of how you use them, drop shots can be an effective way to win points.

THIS CHAPTER HAS COVERED the basics of pickleball, including the different types of serves and shots that can be used. It also touched on some of the key strategies that can be employed in pickleball. In the next chapter, we will take a more in-depth look at pickleball techniques and how to put together a winning game plan. With this knowledge, you should be able to get started playing pickleball and start enjoying this fun and exciting sport. Remember to have fun and practice your strokes and shots so that you can improve your game.

4
TECHNIQUES

Perfecting your pickleball technique can be the difference between winning and losing a match. You can use various techniques in Pickleball, and it is crucial to learn as many as possible to be a well-rounded player. There is much to learn from movement and positioning to advances and defensive techniques. This chapter will discuss some of the most important pickleball techniques that all players should know. By the end, you should have a better understanding of the game and be able to apply these techniques on the court.

Movement and Positioning

One of the key aspects of Pickleball is proper movement and positioning. Players must be strategic in their placement on the court to stay in the best position to return the ball. For example, players may stand closer to the net to put themselves in a better position to make a shot. Or they may back up from the net to give themselves more time to react to their opponent's shot. Regardless of what position players find themselves in, proper movement and positioning are essential for success in Pickleball.

Lateral Movements

If you want to succeed in Pickleball, you need to master lateral movement. This means being able to move quickly and efficiently from side to side to keep up with the ball. You need to focus on a few key elements to do this - and do it safely, without injuring yourself.

FIRSTLY, ensure that you are using your ankles, knees, and hips to generate power. Secondly, keep your center of gravity low so that you can move quickly and easily. Thirdly, practice your footwork by moving side to side while keeping your feet shoulder-width apart. By focusing on these key elements, you will be well on your way to improving your lateral movement and becoming a pickleball champion!

1. Side Steps

ONE OF THE most useful skills in Pickleball is being able to move quickly and efficiently around the court. One way to do this is by learning how to sidestep. Start by planting your feet shoulder-width apart, then lower your center of gravity by bending your knees. From there, shift your weight to your left foot and push off with your right foot, propelling yourself sideways. As you move, keep your feet close to the ground and your head up to see where the ball is going. Practice doing this to strengthen the muscles involved in the movement, and you soon be sidestepping around the court like a pro in no time.

2. Back Pedals

In Pickleball, like tennis and badminton, there are times when you need to backpedal. Perhaps you've made a wrong turn and need to get back to the other side of the court, or maybe your opponent has hit the ball deep, and you need to beat them to the shot. Whatever the reason, being able to backpedal effectively can give you a big advantage in the game.

Start with your stance low, with your feet about shoulder-width apart. This will help you keep your balance as you move backward. Bend your knees and keep your weight on your toes. This will help you generate power as you push off with each step. Take small, quick steps and concentrate on staying light on your feet. The key is maintaining your balance and not letting your feet get ahead of your body.

The key to a successful backpedal is to keep your eyes focused on where you want to go. This will help you stay aware of your surroundings and avoid obstacles. Stay relaxed and use your arms for balance. If you start to feel tense, it will be harder to move quickly and change direction if necessary.

3. Crossover Steps

. . .

CROSSOVER STEPS ARE a great way to keep your opponent guessing in Pickleball. Essentially, you are switching the position of your feet as you move around the court. You can do this by crossing one foot over the other or turning your body, so your weight is on the opposite foot from where it started.

CROSSOVER STEPS CAN BE USED to change directions quickly or to create an opening for a shot. They are also an excellent way to stay balanced when moving around the court. To execute a crossover step, simply start by moving one foot behind the other. Then, crossover your back foot so it ends up in front of your leading foot. You can then either push off with your back foot to change directions or use your front foot to take a shot.

Forward Movements

One of the things that makes Pickleball so unique is the forward movement. It allows for shorter rallies and more opportunities to score points. As a result, the game is fast-paced and exciting. Another benefit of the forward movement is that it helps to improve footwork and hand-eye coordination. So Pickleball is a lot of fun and can also help improve your physical skills. Here are some types of forwarding movements that you can use in Pickleball.

1. The Lunge

THE LUNGE IS a great way to move forward quickly and get to the ball. To execute a lunge, start standing with your feet shoulder-width apart. Then, take a large step forward with your right foot and bend your knees, so your left leg is extended behind you. As you lunge forward, reach out with your racket, and hit the ball. Be sure to keep your eyes on the ball to make contact.

2. The Hop

THE HOP IS a great way to move forward and stay light on your feet. Start by bending your knees and lowering your center of gravity to execute a hop. Then, take a small jump forward and land on both feet at the same time. Be sure to keep your knees bent to absorb the impact of the landing. As you hop forward, reach out with your racket, and hit the ball.

3. The Sprint

THE SPRINT IS a great way to move forward quickly and take your opponent by surprise. To execute a sprint, start standing with your feet shoulder-width apart. Then, lower your center of gravity and explode forward. Take long, powerful strides as you run towards the ball. As you get closer, reach out with your racket, and hit the ball. Be sure to keep your eyes on the ball to make contact.

Backward Movements

Backward movements are a great way to stay in the game and keep your opponent guessing. They can be used to change directions quickly or to create an opening for a shot. So not only are they helpful, but they can also be a lot of fun. Here are some types of backward movements that you can use in Pickleball.

1. The Back Pedal

THE BACK PEDAL is a great way to move back quickly and stay in the game. To execute a back pedal, start standing with your feet shoulder-width apart. Then, take a large step backward with your right foot and bend your knees so that your left leg is extended behind you. As you back pedal, reach out with your racket and hit the ball. Be sure to keep your eyes on the ball so that you can make contact.

2. The Backward Crossover

THE BACKWARD CROSSOVER is a great way to change directions quickly and take your opponent by surprise. To execute a backward crossover, start by moving one foot behind the other. Then, crossover your back foot so that it ends up in front of your leading foot. You can then either push off with your back foot to change directions or use your front foot to take a shot.

3. The Backward Hop

THE BACKWARD HOP is a great way to move back quickly and stay light on your feet. To execute a backward hop, start by bending your knees and lowering your center of gravity. Then, take a small jump backward and land on both feet simultaneously. Be sure to keep your knees bent to absorb the impact of the landing. As you hop backward, reach out with your racket, and hit the ball.

Advances Techniques

There are many different ways to play Pickleball, and each player develops their own style. However, there are some advanced techniques that all players should know. These techniques can help you advance your game and gain an advantage over your opponents. Some of the most popular advanced pickleball techniques are listed below.

1. The Drop Shot

THE DROP SHOT is a great way to keep your opponent guessing. Drop shots can be used to win points or defensive moves, depending on the situation. These are low-lying shots that just clear the net, making them hard to reach for your opponent. To execute a drop shot:

1. Start by hitting the ball high into the air.
2. As it starts to come down, hit it with a downward motion so that it just clears the net.
3. Put a spin on the ball so that it doesn't go out of bounds.

2. The Drive

· · ·

THE DRIVE IS a powerful shot that is used to win points. Drives are low-lying shots that travel quickly and don't give your opponent time to react. To execute a drive:

1. Start by hitting the ball high into the air.
2. As it starts to come down, hit it with a downward motion so that it just clears the net.
3. Put a spin on the ball so it doesn't go out of bounds.

3. The Dink

THE DINK IS a soft shot that just clears the net and drops into the backcourt, making it difficult for the opponent to return. Dink shots are an important part of the game because they help keep the rally going and pressure the other team. The key to hitting a successful dink shot is to keep the ball low so that it just clears the net. You can also add spin to the ball to make it more difficult for your opponent to return.

Defense in Pickleball

In Pickleball, defense is just as important as offense. After all, the best way to win a point is not to let your opponent score in the first place! There are a few key things to remember in mind when playing defense. First, always be aware of where the ball is and where your opponents are. This will help you anticipate their shots and be ready to return the ball.

. . .

SECOND, keep your paddle low to the ground. This will help you block more shots and make it harder for your opponents to get the ball past you. Finally, practice your footwork. Quick and agile footwork will help you reach more balls and stay in position to defend your court. By heeding the following tips, you can develop strong defensive skills and frustrate your opponents on the pickleball court.

1. Cover the Middle

WHEN PLAYING PICKLEBALL, one important thing to keep in mind is defense. In particular, cover the middle of the court. This is because the majority of shots will be hit to the middle of the court, and if you're not covering that area, your opponent will have an easy shot. There are a few different ways to cover the middle of the court. One is to stand in the middle of the court and move from side to side as needed.

ANOTHER WAY IS to split step - that is, to take a small step with one foot towards the direction you think your opponent will hit the ball. And finally, you can also back up towards the baseline - this will help you cover more ground and also give you a little more time to react to your opponent's shot.

2. Get Low

. . .

In Pickleball, defense is all about being in the right place at the right time. By positioning yourself properly, you can cut off your opponents' angles and force them to hit the ball where you want it to go. One of the best ways to improve your defense is to get low. By crouching down, you can make it harder for your opponents to hit the ball over your head.

Getting low will help you stay balanced and move quickly from one side of the court to the other. While getting comfortable moving around in a low stance may take some practice, doing so can pay big dividends on the pickleball court. The next time you're playing, make a conscious effort to get low and see how it affects your defensive game.

3. Use Your Feet

Your feet are your best weapon when playing defense in Pickleball. By using quick and agile footwork, you'll cover more ground and make it harder for your opponent to hit the ball. And if you can learn to position yourself correctly, you'll be able to cut off your opponent's angles and force them into making mistakes. So next time you're on the pickleball court, remember to use your feet. With a little practice, you'll be surprised at how much of a difference it can make.

4. Communicate with Your Partner

Communication is one of the most important aspects of Pickleball. When you are on the court with a partner, it is important to be able to talk to each other to make sure that you are both on the same page. There are a few things that you can do to make sure that your communication is effective.

FIRST, make sure you are speaking clearly and loudly enough so your partner can hear you. Second, use hand signals to supplement your verbal communication. This will help to ensure that your partner knows what you are trying to say. Finally, take some time before the game to discuss strategy with your partner. This will help ensure that you are both on the same page and give you a better chance of winning the game.

5. Learn the Third Shot Drop

IN PICKLEBALL, the third shot drop is an essential defensive technique. When your opponents are getting ready to hit their third shot, you should drop your paddle behind the kitchen line so that it's touching the ground. This will block their shot and force them to hit the ball up, giving you a chance to hit it back. Additionally, you should make sure that your paddle is close to the ground so that you can quickly react to their shots. With a little practice, you'll be able to master this essential defensive technique and frustrate your opponents.

THE TECHNIQUE that you use in Pickleball will have a big impact on your success. In this chapter, we discussed how movement and positioning are important in Pickleball. We also discussed the different movement types, advanced techniques, and how to use your feet. Additionally, we discussed the importance of communication and the third shot drop.

By using the right techniques, you can improve your game and make it harder for your opponents to score. So next time you're on the court, put all your training into practice and see how they can help you to win the game.

5

STRATEGIES

As a newcomer to the sport, you must surely wonder what strategies are used to win the game. It may not be as complicated as you think. Pickleball is a game of strategy. The player who can execute the right strategy at the right time often comes out on top. This chapter will look at how successful tactics can help you stand out from the crowd. We'll also explore how to implement these strategies on the pickleball court.

Advantages of Offensive Play

In Pickleball, there are two main types of offensive play: drinking and driving. Dinking is a soft shot that is used to keep the ball in play and force the opponent to move around the court - rather like when the pro tennis players hit the ball softly over the net, forcing their opponent to run like mad to reach it. And like tennis, this shot is usually used when the opponent is at the back of the court and there is no clear opportunity to score a point. On the other hand, driving is much more aggressive than is designed to win points. It involves hitting the ball hard and low over the net, making it difficult for the opponent to return.

While both drinking and driving have advantages, driving is generally considered the more effective offensive strategy. This is because it allows you to take control of the point and put pressure on your opponent. As a result, it is often considered the best way to win points in Pickleball. Here are some more advantages of offensive play:

1. Gives You the First Strike

In Pickleball, the player who serves the ball has the advantage of being able to control the point from the very beginning. However, this doesn't mean that returning players are at a disadvantage. Offensive play can be a powerful tool for taking control of the point. The first strike allows you to put your opponent on the defensive and force them to react to your shots.

By being aggressive and taking the first strike, you force your opponent to react to your shots rather than dictating the pace of the point themselves. This can throw them off their game and give you a significant advantage. Additionally, the offensive play puts pressure on your opponent and can often lead to mistakes. So, if you're looking to take control of the game, don't be afraid to be aggressive and go on the offensive.

. . .

2. Creates Opportunities

When playing offensive, the goal is to put the ball in a place where your opponent can't get to it, forcing them to make an error. This can be achieved by placement and power. Playing offensively can help you take control of the game and create opportunities for you. It can be especially helpful if you are playing against someone better at defending than you are at attacking.

Being more aggressive can force your opponent to make mistakes and open up the court for yourself. Playing offensive can also help to wear your opponent down over time, as they will have to work harder to defend against your attacks. Ultimately, whether you play offensive, or defensive will depend on your strengths and weaknesses as well as those of your opponent. However, keep in mind that being more offensive can definitely give you an edge in Pickleball.

3. Forces Your Opponent to Play Your Style

One of the biggest benefits of offensive play is that it forces your opponent to play to your style. If you constantly attack, your opponent will have to spend more time on the defensive. This will wear them down mentally and physically, making it easier for you to win the match. It keeps your opponent constantly off-balance, and they'll never know what you will do next. This naturally makes it difficult for them to make a strategic decision or stick to their game-plan. As a result, they are more likely to make mistakes, giving you an advantage.

OF COURSE, offensive play is not without its risks. If you are not careful, you can quickly become overextended and leave yourself open to counterattacks. Additionally, aggressive play can sometimes backfire if your opponent can take advantage of your mistakes. However, when used correctly, offensive play can be a powerful tool in Pickleball. It can help you remain in control.

4. Tires Your Opponent Out

ONE OF THE biggest advantages of offensive play is that it tires out your opponent. Constantly chasing after the ball will take its toll, especially in the later rounds when players are already winded. This will give you a significant advantage, as your opponents will have less energy to put into their shots.

AS YOUR OPPONENTS start to feel the fatigue, they will become more likely to make unforced errors. Therefore, by keeping up a strong offensive game, you can wear down your opponents and put yourself in a better position to win.

5. Get into a Rhythm Quicker

IF YOU ARE PLAYING Pickleball and are stuck in the backcourt, it can be difficult to get into a rhythm and start scoring points.

However, if you take an offensive approach and play at the net, you can get that rhythm going much quicker. When you are offensive, you control the game and can dictate the pace. This can be especially helpful if you are playing against a more defensive opponent. If you want to get into a rhythm quickly and start scoring points, take an offensive approach to your pickleball game.

Power Play

In Pickleball, "power play" is a strategy in which the player tries to hit hard and deep shots to win the point. This can be effective if the player has the strength and skills to hit the ball with power. Additionally, the power play can help to tire out the opponent, as they will have to run back and forth across the court.

WHEN TO USE a **Power Play**

IN PICKLEBALL, a power play is when you use your service to put your opponent on the defensive, setting yourself up for an easy shot. Power plays can be useful when you're behind in the score and need to catch up quickly or when you're trying to take control of the game.

THERE ARE a few things to keep in mind when using a power play. First, ensure you have a good grip on your paddle and are standing in the proper position. Secondly, hit the ball hard and low over the net so that it bounces high on your opponent's side. Finally, be ready to take your shot as soon as your opponent returns the ball. When used correctly, power plays can give you a big advantage in Pickleball.

How to Execute a Power Play

POWER PLAYS ARE an essential part of Pickleball, and there are a few different ways to execute them. The most important thing is to have a clear plan and to be able to play it out quickly. One way to do this is to set up a power-play is to hit the ball really hard and low over the net. This will force your opponents to back up, giving you more space to work with.

ANOTHER OPTION IS to hit the ball deep into the back of your opponent's court, which will make it harder for them to reach it and allow you to set up a shot. Finally, you can also use a drop shot as a power play. This involves hitting the ball softly and high over the net, forcing your opponents to come forward. If you can master these power plays, you'll be well on your way to success in Pickleball.

Defensive Strategies

Defensive strategies, as the name suggests, are used to keep your opponent from scoring and for you to control the court. There are a few key defensive strategies that can be used in Pickleball. First, always try to keep your paddle in front of you. This will help you block the ball and keep it from going past you.

. . .

SECOND, try to stay low and level with your paddle. This will help you keep the ball close to the ground and make it more difficult for your opponent to return it. Finally, be sure to practice your footwork. Proper footwork will allow you to quickly move around the court and stay in position to make plays.

BY USING the following defensive strategies, you can greatly improve your chances of winning pickleball games:

1. Stay Back

ONE OF THE most important defensive strategies is to stay back. This will help you to cover more of the court and makes it more difficult for your opponent to hit the ball past you. In addition, staying back gives you more time to react to your opponent's shots. Practicing the footwork will give you the physical dexterity you need to quickly move side to side and stay in position.

2. Attack Softly

ANOTHER STRATEGY IS to attack softly. This involves hitting the ball softly and high over the net. Your opponent will then have to come forward to return the ball, allowing you to take control of the court. Be sure to practice your drop shots so that you can execute this strategy correctly.

. . .

3. Use Your Opponent's Force against Them

A THIRD DEFENSIVE strategy is to use your opponent's force against them. This can be done by hitting the ball off of their paddle with your own. The force of their shot will then be redirected back at them, making it more difficult for them to control the ball. If you can master this technique, you'll be one step ahead of your opponent.

4. Use the Entire Court

A FOURTH DEFENSIVE strategy is to use the entire court. This means moving around the court and using all of your available space. Using the line is a great way to defend your side of the court. Aim for the line on your opponent's side when you hit the ball. Doing this will make it more difficult for your opponent to predict where you'll be and what shots you'll make.

5. Vary Your Shots

FINALLY, it is critical to vary your shots. This will keep your opponent on their toes and make it difficult for them to defend against you. Attempt to vary your shot selection to keep your opponent guessing. If you can do this, you'll be well on your way to Pickleball success.

Line Double Strategy

If you're looking for a pickleball strategy that will help you take control of the game, then you should try the line double. By committing to the baseline and positioning yourself on either side of the center line, you'll be in a prime position to field any shots that come your way. And, because you'll have two people at the baseline, you'll also be able to cover more ground and put pressure on your opponents.

THIS STRATEGY CAN BE ESPECIALLY effective if you have a strong player at the net, as they'll be able to pounce on any weak shots that come their way. The aim is to keep the ball in play and make it difficult for your opponents to return it.

YOU'LL NEED to practice your footwork and communication with your partner to successfully execute this strategy. You'll also need to have a good understanding of the line on the court. By using the double line strategy, you can take control of the game and put your opponents on the defensive.

Mid-Court Strategy

The mid-court strategy is another great way to control the court. This involves hitting the ball to the middle of the court, forcing your opponents to split their attention between the two sides. To successfully execute this strategy, you'll need to have good communication with your partner. You'll also need to be able to hit the ball accurately to the middle of the court. If you can do this, points and victory are going to be flying your way.

. . .

This chapter has covered a lot of ground and hopefully has given you some useful strategies to improve your game. Now you know the advantages of offensive play, the different types of defensive strategies, and how to use the line to your advantage. With these strategies, you will be well on your way to success in Pickleball. Be sure to practice them so that you can master them. By using these strategies, you can take control of the game and put your opponents on the defensive.

6

MISTAKES TO AVOID IN PICKLEBALL

When playing Pickleball, it is essential to avoid making common mistakes that can cost you the game. Some of the most common mistakes include poor serving, inconsistent volleying, and failing to stay hydrated. By avoiding these mistakes, you can improve your game and increase your chances of winning. In this chapter, we will discuss some of the common pickleball mistakes and how to avoid them.

Serving Mistakes

There are no second chances when it comes to serving. The point is immediately awarded to your opponent if you make a serving mistake. That's why you must practice regularly before stepping onto the court. With a little practice, you'll be able to avoid those costly mistakes and have more fun on the court. Here are some common serving mistakes and ways to avoid them:

. . .

1. Not Keeping the Ball Low

One of the most common serving mistakes is not keeping the ball low. When you hit the ball too high, it gives your opponent time to set up their shots and makes it easier for them to return the ball. Not only that but hitting the ball too high also makes it harder for you to control your shots. To avoid this mistake, remember to keep your ball low when serving. This way, you'll be able to take your opponents by surprise and give yourself a better chance of winning the point.

2. Poor Footwork

Another common serving mistake is poor footwork. When you don't have the correct footwork, generating power and controlling your shots is difficult. As a result, your serves will often be weak and easy for your opponents to return. To avoid this mistake, make sure to practice your footwork before serving. This way, you'll be able to move more easily and hit the ball with more power.

3. Not Focusing on Your Target

When serving, focus on your target. If you don't focus on where you want the ball to go, your service will likely end up in the net or out of bounds. Take a few moments to concentrate on your target before delivering so you don't make this error. Using this technique, you'll be able to hit your service where you want it to go.

4. Hitting the Ball Too Hard

Hitting the ball too hard is another common serving mistake. When you hit the ball too hard, it's difficult to control your shots. As a result, your serves will often be wild and unpredictable. This can give your opponents an easy point. To avoid making this, remember to hit the ball with controlled power. This approach will help you keep your shots under control while also increasing your chances of winning the point.

5. Inconsistent Contact Point

When serving, try to have a consistent contact point. If your contact point is inconsistent, your serves will be less accurate and more likely to land out of bounds. To avoid this problem, take some time to practice your serves. This way, you'll be able to find a consistent contact point and deliver more accurate serves.

Volleying Mistakes

Volleying is an integral part of Pickleball and can be the difference between winning and losing a point. However, many players make common mistakes when volleying. These mistakes can cost you the point and leave you feeling frustrated. Here are some of the most common volleying mistakes and how to avoid them:

1. Not Being Aggressive Enough

One of the most common volleying mistakes is not being aggressive enough. Be aggressive when volleying to avoid this blunder. When you're not aggressive, it's easy for your opponents to return your shots. Not only that, but it also gives them time to set up their shots. By doing this, you'll be able to take your opponents by surprise and give yourself a better chance of winning the point.

2. Not Anticipating Your Opponent's Shots

Another common volleying mistake is not anticipating your opponent's shots. When you don't anticipate their shots, they can easily return your volley. To avoid making this mistake, take a moment to watch your opponents before hitting the ball. This way, you'll be able to predict their next move and adjust your shot accordingly.

3. Getting Caught in No Man's Land

"No man's land" is the area between the baseline and the service line. This area is often referred to as "the danger zone" because it's difficult to hit shots from this position. Many players make the mistake of getting caught in no man's land when volleying. When you're in this position, it's easy for your opponents to hit the ball past you. To avoid this error, stay close to the baseline when volleying. This way, you'll be better positioned to return their shots.

4. Playing Too Close to the Net

Another common volleying mistake is playing too close to the net. Playing too close to the net makes it easy for your opponents to lob the ball over you. Not only that, but it also gives them a better chance of hitting an angled shot. To avoid this mistake, stay back from the net when volleying. This way, you'll be in a better position to defend against their shots.

5. Not Taking Time to Set Up Your Shot

One of the most important aspects of volleying is taking

the time to set up your shot. Many players make the mistake of hitting the ball before they're ready. When doing this, it's easy to miss or hit the ball out of bounds. To avoid making this mistake, take a moment to set up your shot before hitting the ball. This way, you'll be able to deliver a more accurate volley.

Miscues

1. Foot Faults

A foot fault is called when you hit the ball while your feet are not properly positioned. This can happen if you step on the line or if you cross over into your opponent's court. When this happens, it's called a "fault." Foot faults can be costly because they give your opponent's easy free points. Keep your feet properly positioned when serving; this way, you'll be less likely to make a foot fault.

2. Let Serves

A let serve is a serve that hits the net and then lands in bounds. This can happen if the wind blows the ball into the net or if the ball hits a branch. When this happens, it's called a "let." Let serves give your opponents a free point. To avoid this mistake, be careful when serving in windy conditions. This way, you'll be less likely to hit a let serve.

3. Double Hits

A double hit occurs when you hit the ball more than once. This can happen if you hit the ball with your racquet and then with your body or if you hit the ball twice with your racquet. When this happens, it's called a "fault." Hold your racquet readily in one hand when hitting the ball to avoid double hitting. This way, you'll be less likely to hit the ball twice.

4. Unforced Errors

An unforced error is a mistake you make without your opponent's help. This happens if you hit the ball out of bounds or into the net. When this happens, it's called an "error." If you make too many unforced errors, it will be challenging to win the game. To avoid making this mistake, focus on making good shots. Don't try to hit the ball too hard. Just focus on making good, solid contact.

5. Overheads

Overhead is a shot you hit while the ball is above your head. This can be a difficult shot because it's hard to control where the ball will go. Many players make the mistake of hitting the ball too hard when they hit an overhead. When you do this, it's likely the ball will fly out of bounds. If you make this mistake, focus on making good contact with the ball to control where it goes.

Equipment Related Mistakes

When playing Pickleball, it is essential to have the right equipment. Otherwise, you will not be able to play at your best. Here are some of the most common mistakes people make when choosing their pickleball equipment:

- **Not Playing with the Right Paddle:** The paddle is one of the most important pieces of equipment in Pickleball. If you are not using the right paddle,

you will not be able to hit the ball properly. Make sure to choose a paddle that is the right size and weight.
- **Not Wearing the Right Shoes:** Wearing the wrong shoes can impact your game in several ways. First, you may not have enough traction, which can cause you to slip and fall. Second, you may not have enough support, leading to ankle and knee problems. Make sure to choose a shoe that is designed for Pickleball and gives you adequate support and traction.
- **Pickleball is an active sport, and you will be moving around a lot.** As such, it is essential to wear comfortable clothing that allows you to move freely. Avoid loose-fitting clothing that can hamper your movement. Choose loose-fitting clothing that won't restrict your movement.
- **Using the Wrong Balls:** If you are using the wrong balls, you will not be able to play at your best. Make sure to choose balls that are the right size, weight, and hardness for your skill level.

It is important to properly maintain your equipment if you want it to last. This means cleaning your paddle after each use and storing it in a safe place. It also means regularly checking your balls for wear and tear and replacing them when necessary.

General Mistakes

1. Getting Frustrated

One common mistake that pickleball players make is getting frustrated when things don't go their way. It's important to remember that Pickleball is a game and is meant to be enjoyed. Getting angry or upset will only make the game less enjoyable for both you and your opponents. If you find yourself getting frustrated, try to take a deep breath and relax. Focus on having fun and playing the best you can.

2. Losing Concentration

One of the most common mistakes made in Pickleball is losing concentration. When you lose focus, you start making mental errors that can cost you the game. It's easy to get caught up in the excitement of the game and forget to stay focused, but it's important to keep your mind on the task at hand.

IF YOU FIND yourself losing concentration, take a deep breath and try to refocus on the game. Additionally, avoid getting distracted by spectators or other players. If you can stay focused and avoid making mental mistakes, you'll be well on your way to winning pickleball games.

3. Not Staying Hydrated

One of the most common mistakes players make in Pickleball is not staying hydrated. While it may not seem like a big deal, dehydration can lead to cramping, mental fog, and a loss of energy. As a result, it's important to drink plenty of fluids before, during, and after pickleball games or practice sessions. Water is always the best choice, but sports drinks can also be good for replenishing electrolytes.

4. Not Being Prepared

Another error that some players make is not being

prepared mentally and physically for their games. Pickleball is a fast-paced game, and it's easy to pull a muscle if you're not warmed up properly. Warming up and stretching properly before playing, so your muscles are loose and relaxed is essential. A simple warm-up routine of a light jog or some dynamic stretching can help to reduce the risk of injury. You should also take some time to visualize the game to know what you need to do to succeed.

5. Not Playing to Your Strengths

One of the biggest mistakes people make is not playing to their strengths. For example, if you have a strong backhand, you should focus on using that to your advantage. Instead, many people try to play around with their weaknesses, which only serves to give their opponents an advantage.

THIS CHAPTER HAS OUTLINED some of the most common mistakes made in Pickleball. While avoiding all of them is impossible, being aware of these mistakes can help you avoid them in your own game. Remember to stay focused, hydrated, and prepared and play to your strengths. With these tips in mind, you'll be well on your way to playing your best Pickleball.

7
THE WORLD PICKLEBALL GAMES

The World Pickleball Games are one of the most significant events on the pickleball calendar. If you haven't heard of it, the World Pickleball Games is an international pickleball tournament that is held every two years. More than just a tournament, the World Pickleball Games is a week-long event that includes clinics, exhibitions, and social events.

WITH ATHLETES COMING from all over the world to compete, the World Pickleball Games are truly a global event. This chapter will provide an overview of the World Pickleball Games, including when and where they are held, who can compete, and what events are contested. You'll also learn about the benefits of competing in the World Pickleball Games.

What Are the World Pickleball Games?

Pickleball Games are a chance for pickleball players from all over the world to compete against each other. The World Pickleball Games are open to players of all skill levels, and the competition is divided into divisions based on age and experience. The last World Pickleball Games are scheduled for 2023. If you love Pickleball, then the World Pickleball Games are a must-attend event.

THE HISTORY of the World Pickleball Tournaments

FOR MANY PEOPLE, the game of Pickleball is a relatively new sport. However, the origins of pickleball date back to the 1960s, when the game was invented by three dads looking for a way to keep their kids entertained. The game quickly gained popularity, and by the 1970s, an estimated 200,000 people played pickleball in the United States.

IN 1976, the first official pickleball tournament was held in Florida, and since then, the game has continued to grow in popularity. Today, an estimated 3 million people play Pickleball around the world. In 2022, there will be over 100 tournaments scheduled to take place worldwide, including the World Pickleball Games. The game is particularly popular among seniors as it is a low-impact indoor or outdoor sport.

IN THE UNITED STATES, the game of Pickleball is governed by the USA Pickleball Association (USAPA). The USAPA was founded in 1984 and is responsible for promoting the game of

Pickleball, organizing tournaments, and sanctioning events. Whether you're a seasoned player or just getting started, the World Pickleball Games is an event that you won't want to miss.

MEMBER COUNTRIES

OVER 34 COUNTRIES are expected to be represented at the 2023 World Pickleball Games. Some of the member countries include the United States, Australia, Argentina, England, France, Canada, and Italy. Some of the athletes that are expected to compete in the World Pickleball Games have won medals at previous Olympic Games. This includes athletes from the United States, Australia, and Canada.

THE WORLD PICKLEBALL Games is more than just a tournament; it is a chance for countries to come together and compete in a friendly and international event. Many newer countries have also proposed teams, including India, South Africa, and Mexico. These countries are quickly developing pickleball programs and are expected to be competitively represented in the World Pickleball Games.

EVENTS

THE WORLD PICKLEBALL Games include both singles and doubles tournaments. There are also mixed doubles tournaments, where men and women compete on the same team. In addition to the traditional tournament events, some exhibitions and clinics take place during the week-long event.

THE EXHIBITION MATCHES are a chance for the top pickleball players in the world to showcase their skills in a non-competitive setting. These matches are often played against each other, and the exhibition is a great way to see some of the best pickleball players in the world.

THE CLINICS ARE another opportunity for attendees to learn more about the game of Pickleball. These clinics are led by some of the world's top pickleball players and instructors. Attendees will have the chance to learn about different techniques, strategies, and skills that can help them improve their game.

QUALIFYING for the World Pickleball Games

THE WORLD PICKLEBALL Games are open to all pickleball players from around the world. However, there is a qualification process that players must go through to compete.

PLAYERS CAN QUALIFY for the World Pickleball Games by competing in sanctioned tournaments. These tournaments are organized by the USAPA and are held throughout the year. The top players from these tournaments will earn points, and the players with the most points at the end of the qualifying period will earn a spot in the World Pickleball Games.

. . .

IN ADDITION TO THE TOURNAMENTS, players can also qualify by competing in their country's national pickleball championships. The top players from these events will also earn spots in the World Pickleball Games. Whether you're a seasoned player or just getting started, the World Pickleball Games is an event that you won't want to miss.

COMPETITION FORMAT

THE WORLD PICKLEBALL Games is a single-elimination tournament. This means that players are eliminated from the tournament once they lose a match. The tournament will continue until only one player or team remains, who will be crowned the champion.

IN THE SINGLES TOURNAMENT, players compete against each other individually. In the doubles tournament, teams of two players compete against each other. The mixed doubles tournament is an event where teams of one man and one woman compete against each other. This is a relatively new event and was first introduced at the 2017 World Pickleball Games.

SANCTIONING

THE INTERNATIONAL OLYMPIC COMMITTEE sanctions the World Pickleball Games. The IOC is the governing body for the Olympic Games and is responsible for approving new sports for the Olympics. This is a huge step for the sport of Pickleball, and it gives the games an added level of legitimacy.

WHILE PICKLEBALL IS NOT CURRENTLY an Olympic sport, the IOC recognition is a big step in the right direction. It shows that the sport of Pickleball is growing and becoming more popular on a global scale. The future of Pickleball is looking very bright, and the World Pickleball Games are a big part of that.

WORLD PICKLEBALL GAMES **Rule Book**

THE GAME of Pickleball is governed by a set of rules designed to promote fair play and safety. The official rule book for the World Pickleball Games is available online and outlines all the specific regulations that players must follow. For instance, the book explains how the court should be set up, what type of equipment is allowed, and how points are scored.

IN ADDITION, the rule book also includes a code of conduct section outlining expectations for players and spectators alike. The World Pickleball Games is a competitive event, but the games are meant to be fun. Players and spectators are expected to treat each other with respect, and any type of unsportsmanlike conduct will not be tolerated.

. . .

By familiarizing yourself with the World Pickleball Games Rule Book, you can help ensure that everyone has an enjoyable and safe experience at the Games.

Benefits of Competing in the World Pickleball Games

The sport has been around for over 50 years and has since grown in popularity to become one of the most popular racket sports in the world. For many people, the appeal of Pickleball lies in its simple rules and easy-to-learn scoring system. However, the sport also offers several benefits for those who compete at the highest levels. The World Pickleball Games is one of the largest and most prestigious pickleball tournaments in the world and competing in it can offer several benefits.

1. Offers Opportunities

The World Pickleball Games are a great way to improve your skills and make new friends. For starters, the Games offer a unique opportunity to compete against some of the best players in the world. In addition, the Games provide a chance to meet other pickleball enthusiasts from all over the globe and learn about different cultures. It's also an excellent opportunity to see some amazing places, as the Games are held in various locations around the world each year.

2. Significant Financial Benefits

Second, the prize money at stake can provide a significant financial boost for those who can reach the later rounds of the competition. In 2017, the prize money for the singles and doubles tournaments was $20,000 each. The mixed doubles tournament had a prize purse of $10,000. So, it's definitely worth trying out!

3. Improved Skills and Experience

Competing in the World Pickleball Games can be a great way to improve your skills and experience. After all, the best way to get better at anything is to practice against people who are better than you. By competing in the World Pickleball Games, you'll have the opportunity to do just that. You'll be able to test your skills against some of the best pickleball players in the world and see how you stack up. And even if you don't win, you'll still come away with valuable experience that you can use to improve your game.

4. Boosts Confidence

Competing in the world pickleball games can be highly beneficial, especially when it comes to boosting confidence. Competing in these games provides players with a sense of accomplishment and boosts their self-esteem. This is especially important for young players who are still developing their confidence.

5. Chance to Socialize

Competing in the world pickleball games also gives players a chance to meet other people from all over the world and learn about new cultures. This can be a great way to develop new friendships and expand one's worldview. Ultimately, competing in the world pickleball games can be an incredibly enriching experience that can positively impact a person's life far beyond the court.

. . .

6. Help Raise the Profile of Pickleball

Competing in the World Pickleball Games will help to raise the profile of Pickleball as a whole, which can lead to more opportunities for other players in the future. Since the Games are one of the world's biggest and most prestigious pickleball tournaments, players who do well can help put Pickleball on the map and attract more attention to the sport.

7. Fun and Exciting

Last but not least, competing in the World Pickleball Games is simply a lot of fun. It's an exciting event that offers players a chance to show off their skills and compete against some of the best in the world. If you're a competitive person, then there's no doubt that you'll enjoy the challenge of the World Pickleball Games.

Volunteering at the World Pickleball Games

Have you ever considered volunteering at the World Pickleball Games? It's a great way to get involved with the sport and meet other pickleball enthusiasts worldwide. Plus, it's a great way to give back to the sport you love.

THERE ARE a variety of volunteer roles available at the World Pickleball Games, so there's sure to be something that's a perfect fit for you. For example, you could help with set-up and break-down, assist with scoring or officiating, or help with player registration. Whatever role you choose, you'll be an important part of making the World Pickleball Games a success.

· · ·

If you're interested in volunteering at the World Pickleball Games, be sure to fill out a volunteer application form online. And don't forget to spread the word to your pickleball friends - the more volunteers we have, the better the Games will be.

Getting Updates about the World Pickleball Games

If you are interested in getting updates about the world of pickleball games, there are a few different ways to do so. Staying informed about the Pickleball World Games is easy, regardless of which method you choose. One option is to follow the official Pickleball World Games Facebook page. This page regularly posts news and updates about upcoming tournaments, results from recent events, and other information related to the sport of Pickleball.

Another option is to sign up for the Pickleball World Games newsletter. This newsletter is emailed and will keep you up-to-date on all the latest pickleball news and provide information about special events and ticket sales. Finally, you can also visit the official website for the Pickleball World Games. This site provides detailed information about the event, including a schedule of matches, results from previous years, and player profiles.

The World Pickleball Games is a tournament open to players from all over the world. It offers a chance for pickleball enthusiasts to represent their country on a global stage and compete against some of the best players in the sport. In addition to being a great way to showcase one's skills, the World Pickleball Games also offer several other add-ons, such as the opportunity to learn about new cultures and make new friends from all over the world.

If you're interested in competing in the World Pickleball Games, be sure to sign up early and start training for the event. Don't forget to follow the official Pickleball World Games Facebook page and sign up for the email newsletter to stay up-to-date on all the latest news and information.

8

HOW TO PRACTICE BY YOURSELF OR WITH A PARTNER

Playing Pickleball by yourself or with a partner can be fun and, naturally, is a great way to improve your skills. While not everyone may be available to play with you all the time, there are still plenty of ways that you can practice and improve your game. If you are looking to practice on your own or with a friend, this chapter will provide some tips and ideas.

IN THIS CHAPTER, you will learn about using a ball machine, playing wall ball, hitting against a backboard, training with a coach, solo drills, playing point games, playing in tournaments, and more. This chapter will also provide tips on how to improve your game. By the end of this chapter, you will have a better understanding of how to practice Pickleball and improve your skills.

Practicing by Yourself

It can be challenging to find someone to play Pickleball with. You may not have any friends interested in the sport, or you may live in an area where there aren't any pickleball courts. Fortunately, it's possible to practice Pickleball by yourself. While you won't be able to enjoy the competitive aspect of the game, solo practice can still give you a good workout.

HERE ARE some ways to practice Pickleball by yourself:

1. **Using a Ball Machine**

One of the best ways to do this is to use a ball machine. Ball machines can be customized to simulate different types of gameplay, and they provide a consistent, reliable partner you can practice with at any time again and again. Another benefit of using a ball machine is that it allows you to focus on specific skills without being distracted by other players.

IF YOU'RE WORKING on your serve, you can set the machine to deliver balls to the same spot over and over again. This way, you can focus on perfecting your technique. So, if you're looking for a way to take your pickleball game to the next level, using a ball machine is worth considering.

2. **Playing Wall Ball**

Wall ball is another great way to practice Pickleball by yourself. Wall ball involves hitting the ball against a wall, either with your hand or with a paddle. The goal is to keep the ball in the air for as long as possible. Not only does this help you improve your hand-eye coordination, but it also gives you a chance to work on your power and accuracy.

To make the most of your wall ball practice, try to find a wall that is smooth and flat. This will give you the best bounce and help you get the most out of your practice. You can also use a wall that is painted with pickleball lines to help you improve your aim. Playing wall ball is a great way to warm up before a game or practice session. So next time you're looking for something to do by yourself, grab a pickleball paddle and head to the nearest wall.

3. Hitting against a Backboard

Hitting against a backboard is another great way to practice your pickleball skills. Backboards are large, flat surfaces often used in tennis, but they can be just as effective for Pickleball. Hitting against a backboard allows you to work on your power and accuracy. It also allows you to practice your strokes without worrying about where the ball is going.

A backboard is a great alternative to hitting against a wall since it provides a consistent surface and target to hit the ball against and stability. This can help you focus on your technique and hone your skills. To get the most out of your backboard practice, try to find a backboard that is made of smooth, durable material. Hit the ball exactly in the center of the board for the best results.

4. Training with a Coach

If you're serious about taking your pickleball game to the

next level, then training with a coach is something you should consider. A coach can help you identify your weaknesses and work on them. They can also give you feedback on your technique and offer tips on how to improve. The best part about training with a coach is that they can tailor your workouts to your specific needs.

TRAINING WITH A COACH is not always possible, but it is worth considering if you have the opportunity. If you don't have a coach, you can try attending pickleball clinics or taking private lessons. These can be expensive, but they will give you the chance to get one-on-one instruction from a professional. With a little bit of effort, you can find a pickleball coach that is right for you.

5. Solo Drills

If you're looking to improve your pickleball skills, solo drills are a great way to focus on specific areas of your game. By doing drills by yourself, you can control the speed and placement of the ball, and you can also take as much time as you need to perfect your technique. Plus, solo drills are a great way to stay motivated and improve your stamina. Here are some pickleball solo drills that you can try:

A GREAT SOLO drill is the "around-the-world" drill. This drill helps you work on your reaction time and hand-eye coordination. To do this drill, start by hitting the ball against a wall. As the ball comes back to you, hit it again so that it goes in a different direction. Keep hitting the ball around the court until it comes back to the starting point.

· · ·

THE DROP SHOT solo drill is also a great way to work on your accuracy and control. However, you'll need plenty of balls for this. To do this drill, start by hitting the balls over the net into the other court. The goal is to land the ball in the same spot each time. This drill is great for improving your touch and accuracy.

THESE ARE JUST a few of the many solo drills you can do to improve your pickleball skills. When you're practicing by yourself, take the time to focus on your technique and form. This will help you improve your game and become a better pickleball player overall.

Practicing with a Partner

Pickleball is a great game for all ages. It is easy to learn yet challenging enough to keep you coming back for more. One of the best ways to improve your pickleball skills is to practice with a partner. You can work on your shots and placement when you have someone to bounce the ball off. You can also try different angles and speeds to see what works best.

IN ADDITION, practicing with a partner helps you stay focused and motivated. With someone else counting on you, staying on task and practicing regularly is easier. So, if you are looking to improve your pickleball game, find a partner and start practicing. Here are some tips on how to improve your pickleball game by practicing with a partner:

1. **Practicing Your Serves**
    One of the most important strokes in Pickleball is the

serve. A good serve sets up the game, so you gain control from the start and have your opponents on the defensive. When practicing with a partner, it's crucial to take turns serving so that both of you have a chance to work on your serves. Start by standing behind the baseline and serving diagonally into your partner's service box.

YOU CAN EXPERIMENT with different angles and speeds as you get more comfortable with your service. Just keep the ball inside the service box. If you're struggling to get the hang of it, don't worry - even the best pickleball players had to practice their serves before they perfected them.

2. Working on Your Volleys

Keep a few things in mind when working on your volleys. First, make sure you're using the right grip. A Continental grip is best for volleys, as it will give you more control over the ball. Second, be sure to keep your racket head up. This will help you get more power behind your shots. Finally, don't forget to follow through with your swing. This will give the ball plenty of spins and stay on course.

YOUR PARTNER CAN HELP you practice your volleys by standing in the middle of the court and hitting the ball back to you. You can start moving around the court and practicing your volleys from different angles as you get better. Try to keep the ball in play for as long as possible. The longer you can keep the rally going, the better.

3. Improving Your Footwork

Footwork is important in all racquet sports, and Pickleball is no exception. When you're practicing with a partner, set aside time in your session to concentrate and focus on your footwork, this will help you move around the court more efficiently and improve your overall game.

YOU CAN DO the four corners drill to improve your footwork. To do this drill, start in the middle of the court. Then, run to the right corner, the left corner, the back right corner, and finally, the back left corner. Touch each line with your foot as you go. Then, run back to the middle of the court and repeat.

THIS DRILL MAY SEEM SIMPLE, but it's quite challenging. As you get better, you can increase the speed at which you run. Just be sure to focus on your footwork and use proper form.

4. Learn to Position and Communicate

When playing with someone else, you must constantly be aware of their position on the court and adjust your own accordingly. This will help you develop better footwork habits and learn to move more efficiently around the court. In addition, playing with a partner will also force you to communicate and work together as a team. This is an essential skill in Pickleball, as teamwork is often the key to winning.

TO PRACTICE THIS, start by playing some simple points with your partner. Try mixing up your shots and placement as you get more comfortable. This will help you learn to read your partner's positioning and adjust your own game accordingly.

In addition, be sure to communicate with your partner. Let them know where you want them to hit the ball and what shots you're going to make. This will help you develop better communication skills and learn to work as a team.

5. Drilling Your Shots

Drills are a great way to improve your pickleball skills. When you're practicing with a partner, take the time to focus on drilling specific shots. This will help you develop muscle memory and learn to make the shots you want. During your practice sessions, try to focus on one or two shots that you want to improve. For example, you might want to work on your backhand or your serve.

ONE DRILL you can do is the back and forth drill. To do this drill, start by hitting the ball back and forth with your partner. As you get comfortable, start moving around the court and hitting the ball to different areas. This will help you learn to place your shots and develop better control over the ball. As you get better, you can increase the speed at which you hit the ball. Just be sure to focus on your form and technique.

Tips for Improvement

1. Get a Good Racket

If you're looking to improve your game, one of the best things you can do is to invest in a good racket. Pickleball rackets are specifically designed for the game and can provide several benefits. They're typically lighter than tennis rackets, making them easier to swing. In addition, they have a larger sweet spot, which can help you hit the ball more consistently. Another benefit of a good racket is that it can help you generate more power. Investing in a quality racket is a great place to start if you're looking to take your game to the next level.

2. Use the Right Balls

Three main types of balls are used in Pickleball: indoor, outdoor, and composite. Each type has its advantages and disadvantages, so choosing the right one for your level of expertise is crucial. Indoor balls are made of a softer material, which makes them ideal for use on indoor courts with a soft surface. Outdoor balls are usually made of a harder material, making them ideal for outdoor courts with a hard surface.

COMPOSITE BALLS ARE a mix of both indoor and outdoor balls and can be used on either type of court. Regardless of the type of ball you choose, make sure to practice with it before using it in a game. This will help you get used to the feel of the ball, tweak your game, and improve your accuracy. A good tip is to practice with different types of balls to see which one you prefer.

3. Practice a Variety of Shots

Anyone who's played Pickleball knows that there's more to the game than just hitting the ball over the net. The best players can control the game's pace and keep their opponents guessing using a variety of shots. In Pickleball, there are many different ways to hit the ball, and each shot has its strengths and weaknesses. By practicing various shots, you'll be able to better adapt to the different situations you'll encounter during a match.

. . .

This chapter has provided tips on how to improve your skills when practicing alone or with a partner. Drills are a great way to focus on specific shots and develop muscle memory. In addition, using the right equipment can make a big difference in your game. Practice various shots so you can be prepared for anything during a match.

9

HEALTH AND SAFETY

Pickleball is a sport with many health benefits, but it is also essential to be aware of the potential risks involved in playing. It is recommended and always a wise step to take to consult with your doctor before playing Pickleball, especially if you have any pre-existing medical conditions. This chapter will discuss the health risks and safety considerations associated with Pickleball. It'll also provide some tips on how you can stay safe while playing the game.

Health Risks

As with any sport, there are some health risks associated with Pickleball. The most common injuries are strains and sprains, but more serious injuries can occur if players are not careful and don't warm up properly. The following are some of the potential health risks associated with Pickleball:

1. **Strains and Sprains**

The most common injuries in Pickleball are strains and sprains. These can be caused by overuse of muscles or joints, improper warm-up, or incorrect form when playing. In severe cases, strains and sprains can lead to tendinitis caused by repetitive motion. It is common for tendinitis to develop in the shoulders, elbows, or wrists.

2. Joint Injuries

Joint injuries are also a risk in Pickleball. The repetitive motion of swinging a paddle can stress the joints, leading to inflammation or even arthritis. Players with pre-existing joint problems should be particularly careful when playing Pickleball.

3. Muscle Injuries

Muscle injuries can also occur while playing Pickleball. The most common type of muscle injury is a hamstring strain caused by overstretching the muscle. Other types of muscle injuries include groin strains and calf strains.

4. Head Injuries

Head injuries are a potential risk in any sport, and Pickleball is no exception. The most common type of head injury in Pickleball is a concussion, which can happen if a player gets hit in the head with a ball or paddle. Concussions can cause headaches, nausea, dizziness, and confusion. More serious head injuries, such as skull fractures and brain damage, can also occur but are significantly less common in this sport.

5. Heat-Related Injuries

Pickleball is a strenuous activity, and players can quickly become overheated, especially in hot weather. Heat-related injuries such as heat stroke can occur if the body temperature rises too high. Symptoms of heat stroke include confusion, dizziness, headache, nausea, and vomiting. Players who are not used to playing in hot weather are at a higher risk for heat-related injuries.

Safety Risks

There are a few safety considerations to keep in mind when playing Pickleball. The following are some potential safety risks associated with the sport:

1. Paddle Risks

One of the most important safety considerations in Pickleball is the risk of being hit by a paddle. Paddles are made of hard materials such as wood or a composite, and they can cause serious injuries if players are not careful. Paddle strokes are the most common type of injury in Pickleball, and they can cause bruises, cuts, and even concussions.

2. Ball Risks

Another safety consideration in Pickleball is the risk of being hit by a ball. Pickleballs are made of hard materials such as rubber or plastic, and they can cause serious injuries if players are not careful. Ball strikes are the second most common type of injury in Pickleball, and they can cause bruises, cuts, and even concussions that have been known to occur.

. . .

3. Equipment Risks

Another safety consideration in Pickleball is the risk of using defective or damaged equipment. Pickleball paddles and balls are made of hard materials and can break if they are not properly made or maintained. Defective or damaged paddles and balls can cause serious injuries if players are not careful.

4. Weather Risks

Weather conditions can also be a safety consideration in Pickleball. Hot weather can cause heat-related injuries, and cold weather can cause hypothermia. Wet weather can make pickleball courts slippery and dangerous. Players should always check the weather forecast before playing Pickleball and take appropriate precautions based on the conditions. Players should also wear weather-appropriate shoes to be safe.

5. Court Risks

Pickleball courts can also be a safety issue. Courts in poor condition can be dangerous, and players can suffer injuries if they slip or trip on a court that is in bad shape. Players should always check the condition of the court before playing, and they should avoid playing on courts that have degraded, become slippery, or are generally in poor condition.

6. Collisions

Collisions are another potential safety risk in Pickleball. Players can collide with each other, with the net, or with objects on the court. Collisions can cause injuries such as bruises, cuts, and concussions. These injuries can be prevented by being aware of your surroundings and avoiding collisions.

7. Poor Lighting

Poor lighting can also be a safety consideration in Pickleball. Courts that are not properly lit can be dangerous, and players can suffer injuries if they cannot see where they are going. Players should always check the lighting before playing, and they should avoid playing on courts that are not well lit.

Steps to Stay Safe While Playing Pickleball

Players can take a few steps to stay safe while playing Pickleball. The following are some tips for staying safe while playing the sport:

1. Use the Right Equipment

One of the best ways to stay safe while playing Pickleball is to use the right equipment. Make sure your racket is the correct size and weight for you and that the grip is comfortable. Wear shoes that provide good support and have non-marking soles to avoid slipping. Use a ball that is the correct size and hardness for the type of game you are playing.

To HELP PREVENT COMMON INJURIES, wear proper equipment. For example, elbow pads can help to reduce the risk of tendinitis, while wrist braces can help to protect against fractures. By taking some simple precautions, you can enjoy Pickleball without putting your health at risk.

. . .

2. Warm Up and Cool Down

Warming up before playing Pickleball can help prevent injuries. Start by doing some gentle stretching exercises to loosen your muscles. Then, do some light aerobic activity to get your heart rate up. Then do some dynamic stretches that mimic the movements you will be doing in the game. After your game, walk or jog for a few minutes to cool down gradually.

3. Stay Hydrated

Staying hydrated is important for all sports, and Pickleball is no exception. Drink plenty of fluids before, during, and after your pickleball game. Avoid drinking caffeinated or alcoholic beverages. If you start to feel dizzy or lightheaded, take a break and drink some water. It's also a good idea to wear sunscreen and hats to protect yourself from the sun.

4. Be Aware of Your Surroundings

Pay attention to where the other players are and what they're doing. If someone is getting too close to you, move out of the way. Also, be aware of any obstacles in the court. If you're not sure where the ball is going, don't swing your racket. By being aware of your surroundings, you can help avoid accidents and injuries.

5. Follow the Rules

Pickleball has a set of rules that players are expected to follow. These rules are in place to help keep players safe. For example, the rule about not hitting the ball over the net more than once helps prevent players from colliding with each other. To help keep everyone safe, make sure you follow the rules of Pickleball.

6. Take Breaks

If you start to feel tired, take a break. It's crucial to listen to your body and know your limits. If you push yourself too hard, you could end up injured. Instead, take a break when you need to and come back refreshed. A good rule is taking a break after every game or set. You can also take a break every 20 minutes or so if you're playing an extended game.

7. Check the Court before Playing

Make sure the court is in good condition before you start playing. Look for cracks or uneven surfaces that could trip you up. Also, make sure the net is the correct height and that there are no sharp objects on the court. By taking a few minutes to check the court, you can help avoid accidents and injuries.

8. Play with People You Know

Playing with people you know and trust is always a good idea. That way, you'll be more familiar with their playing style and less likely to get injured. If you're playing with people you don't know, make sure you're aware of their skill level so you can adjust your playing style accordingly.

9. Know Your Limits

Don't try to do more than you're physically capable of. Don't do it if you're uncomfortable making a certain move. Also, be aware of your skill level and play accordingly. In other words, don't try to keep up with the more experienced players if you're a beginner. Knowing your limits will help you stay safe on the court.

10. Be Prepared for the Worst

Even if you take all the necessary precautions, accidents can still happen. It's important to be prepared for the worst. Make sure that a first aid kit is available and that you know where it is and how to use it. You should also know the emergency procedures for the court you're playing on. Preparing for the worst will help you stay safe on the court and boost your confidence.

PICKLEBALL IS a great way to get exercise and have fun. However, it's important to stay safe while playing. First, be sure to use the right equipment. Second, warm up before playing to help prevent injuries. Third, be aware of your surroundings and the other players on the court.

TRY NOT to get in anyone's way, and be careful not to hit anyone with the ball. Finally, always follow the rules of the game. This will help keep everyone safe and ensure that everyone has a good time. By following these simple steps, you can stay safe and have a great time playing Pickleball.

CONCLUSION

Now that you know all about Pickleball, it's time to get out there and start playing! Remember to brush up on the basics, techniques, and strategies listed in this book. And before you head out to the court, hold on and take a look at the winning recipe and recommendations for the best possible experience. This final chapter will conclude the information provided in *Pickleball for Beginners* and also give a final tip.

First and foremost, have fun! Playing Pickleball should be enjoyable, so make sure to find a balance between playing to compete and playing for enjoyment. Of course, there will be some days where you just can't seem to win. On those days, it's important to keep a positive attitude and not get discouraged. This is the winning recipe:

- **Positive Attitude:** No matter what the score is, always try your best and enjoy playing.
- **Determination:** Don't give up and keep practicing improving your skills.

- **Confidence:** Have faith in your abilities and know that you can win.
- **Respect:** For yourself, your opponents, and the game.

Now that you know the winning recipe, here are some recommendations for having the best possible experience while playing Pickleball.

- Invest in good quality pickleball equipment. This includes a paddle, balls, shoes, and clothing. Not only will this improve your game, but it will also make playing more comfortable.
- Find a good pickleball court. The surface, net height, and dimensions of the court can all affect your game.
- Playing with others is the best way to improve your skills and have fun. Find a group of friends or join a pickleball club so you can always have someone to play with.

The first chapter of this book provides an overview of pickleball, including its history and rules. In the second chapter, we covered the basics of pickleball, such as a description of the strokes used and footwork. In the third chapter, we discussed how to get started in pickleball, including finding a court and learning the game. In the fourth chapter, we covered different pickleball techniques, such as how to hit different types of shots.

In the fifth chapter, we discussed different pickleball strategies, such as having an offensive stance and playing doubles. In the sixth chapter, we covered some common mistakes that players make in pickleball. In the seventh chapter, we discussed the World Pickleball Games, which is the biggest pickleball tournament in the world. In the eighth chapter, we discussed how to practice by yourself or with a partner. Finally, in the ninth chapter, we discussed health and safety in pickleball.

The final tip is to never give up. Whether you're just starting, or you've been playing for years, there's always something new to learn. So, keep practicing, stay positive, and most of all, have fun!

GLOSSARY

Volley:
A kick or hit of the pickleball that occurs before it lands.

Non-volley area/zone:
You must wait for a ball to bounce in the zone known as non-volley area/zone before hitting it.

Stalemate:
A circumstance in which it seems difficult for opposing or rival parties to take additional action or make progress.

Tennis elbow:
Pain on the outer of ones elbow seems to be a symptom of tennis elbow. Clinically, it is referred to as lateral-epicondylitis.

USAPA:
Stands for USA-Pickleball-Association

SFIA:

Stands for Sports & Fitness-Industry-Association

SSIPA:

Stands for Super-Senior-International-Pickleball-Association

ASBA:

Stands for American-Sports-Builders-Association

IPTPA:

Stands for International-Pickleball-Teaching-Professional-Association

UTPRs:

Stands for Results-Based-Tournament-Player-Ratings

PPR:

Stands for Professional-Pickleball-Registry

PTR:

Stands for Professional-Tennis-Registry

Middle Shot Drop:

The Middle Shot Drop, which entails a low shot over the net of a pickleball directly into the center of your court, can be the most dependable.

Hard Hit Shot Drop:

For beginner players, a Hard-Hit Shot Drop is a typical go-to move. Hard, elevated, & out of the way are their target objectives.

Intermediate Shot Drop:

You may opt to drill to a net person, down along the line,

Glossary

a lob, side shot drop, dink, or employ a 3rd shot technique in Intermediate Pickleball Shot Drop.

Singles play:
The player must receive their initial serve from the appropriate service court in singles gameplay of Pickleball. Identical to certain other racquet sports, your ball is served towards the opponent's diagonal crosscourt.

Doubles play:
Pickleball doubles gameplay might be a bit harder to follow. The score of serving team, the number of server and the score of receiving team, make up the total. The server number, which may be either 1 or a 2, indicates whether this is the team's first or the second server.

Stacking or Poaching:
Maintain the proper posture of the stronger partner in the Pickleball's game.

Dinking 201:
It involves how to dink the ball while keeping it low; using good footwork will position you for a fantastic dink & when to take the next shot when to do it.

Dinking 101:
To gain court management skills while having a fun.

Defending Lob:
To guard against the terrible lob.

CPSIA information can be obtained
at www.ICGtesting.com
Printed in the USA
BVHW032358271122
652779BV00032B/1040